The Barrio Gangs of San Antonio, 1915–2015

The Barrio Gangs
of San Antonio,
1915–2015

MIKE TAPIA

TCU
Press

FORT WORTH, TEXAS

Library of Congress Cataloging–in–Publication Data

Names: Tapia, Mike, 1974– author.
Title: The barrio gangs of San Antonio, 1915–2015 / Michael A. Tapia. Description: Fort Worth,
Texas : TCU Press, [2017]
Identifiers: LCCN 2016045089 (print) | LCCN 2016045868 (ebook) |
    ISBN 9780875654331 (alk. paper) | ISBN 9780875656489 (alk. paper) |
    ISBN 9780875656649
Subjects: LCSH: Mexican American gangs—Texas—San Antonio—History—20th century. |
    Mexican American criminals—Texas—San Antonio—History—20th century. | San Antonio
    (Tex.)—Social conditions—20th century. Classification: LCC HV6439.U7 T37 2017 (print) |
    LCC HV6439.U7 (ebook) | DDC
364.106089/680764351----dc23
LC record available at https://lccn.loc.gov/2016045089

TCU Box 298300
Fort Worth, Texas 76129
817.257.7822
www.prs.tcu.edu
To order books: 1.800.826.8911

Text Design by Preston Thomas
Cover Design by Isabelle Burke

To Raquel and the kids.
May we continue to share in the joy of our family life.

Contents

Acknowledgments

This book would not have been possible without the assistance of Juan "Chota" Mendoza. Juan vouched for me to his barrio connections, opening the door to many rich and valuable sources of information. He also served as my guide and adviser on the research process throughout. I am fortunate to have crossed paths with this man, whom many in San Antonio know as the "Barrio Historian." As the founder of *Los Barrios Viejos* organization, he was joined by the community in annual celebrations of the lesser-known stories, characters, and triumphs of San Anto's West Side. Thanks Juan. May some of these elements live on through our work together.

Other folks that greatly assisted in the three-year journey of fieldwork, archive collection, organized events, impromptu gatherings and focus groups, etc., were Joe Gallegos Jr., Roy Valdez, Ralph "Philo" Lopez, Marie "Keta" Miranda, and UTSA research assistants Lynsey "La Güera" Tucker, Africa "La Flaca" Young, and Sendy "La Pollita" Tamayo. Thank you all for your faithful assistance, your patience, and for your hard work. I hope this book will always remind you of the friendships we formed and the great times we had in the field.

Last, but certainly not least, I want to thank all of the *vatos* who contributed their time and information to this project. I particularly want to mention Gilbert "Hippo" Carranza, David "Blackie" Anguiano, Rudy Galan, Eddie Ferguson, Pablo and Robert "Los Pilinga" Lopez, "Cool" John Martinez, Alejandro "Lefty" Fuentes, Gilbert Orozco, Norberto "Congo" Soto, Erasmo Mercado, Brigido "Kike" Minjares, Rogelio "Chicken" Garza, Juanillo "Bonne" Lozano, Manuel "El Dracula" Padilla, Apolonio "Rock n Roll" Garcia, Richard "Aleman" Araujo, Chuy Valdez, Chuy Ortegon, Esmeraldo "El Mysterio" Guerra, Pete

"Pio" Tenorio, Jose "Cote" Arias, Mando de los Santos, Nivo Morelli, Quirubin "Kiddo" Espitia (dec), Edward "Popo" Medina (dec), Natividad "Nino" Villarreal (dec), Carlos "Uncs" Alva (dec), El "Black Sam" Rodriguez (dec), and of course, Henry "El Zapatista" Rodriguez.

January 2017

Introduction

Mexican Americans (Chicanos) are the largest ethnic minority group in the United States, and San Antonio, the nation's seventh largest city, is one of the group's biggest population hubs. Where delinquent subcultures are a salient aspect of their communities, the Chicano case has been a significant part of the country's criminological landscape for some time. Yet this particular group is seldom analyzed critically in mainstream crime research. Several exceptions include writings on the *pachuco* genre that developed in the 1930s (Bogardus 1943; Vigil 1988) and the *bandido* subcultures on the Texas-Mexico border that preceded such urban formations (Mirandé 1987). The sociological research on barrio gangs is mainly focused on Southern California groups, without much written on those abundant in Texas. Notable exceptions include the works of David Montejano (2010), and of Avelardo Valdez and coauthors (1999; 2004; 2005; 2009), whose work I draw on here. The current work focuses on urban barrio networks in San Antonio to help fill this gap.

This book examines the genesis of street-corner barrio gang formations going back to about 1910, giving special attention to these groups' heydays from the 1940s through the 1960s. It uses varied qualitative research methods to offer a deeper understanding of barrio gang life than most studies on this topic. It is informed by nearly two decades of field observations, including gang intervention, work experience, and other types of formal study of Latino criminal subcultures in San Antonio. It examines the form and function of delinquent and criminal groups at various stages in their historical development. The intensification of drug trafficking in recent decades provides the modern setting for the growing violence associated with these groups, once thought to be rather normative street-corner societies.

In 1973, the *Texas Monthly* reported on the heroin distribution networks operating along Interstate 35 between San Antonio and Laredo (Moore & Holland 1973). This was followed by Wilson McKinney's groundbreaking book *The Heroin Merchant* (1975). It offered a detailed journalistic profile of a drug-trafficking network mainly comprising Chicanos from San Antonio barrios. Yet, as a snapshot of a brief time period in the city's century-long drug-trafficking dynamic, the work lacked historical context and did not follow future developments in this underworld. These are important gaps in the Texas-based literature on criminal networks that the current work addresses. For example, the murderous tactics employed by these 1960s and '70s drug gangs set a precedent for prison-based gangs in the 1980s, who dominated San Antonio's heroin distribution operations for several decades with violence and intimidation (Valdez 2005).

A younger generation of Chicano prison-to-street hybrids called Tangos came of age in the 2000s. They now compete for respect and a piece of the illegal drug and weapons market in San Antonio and other large Texas cities. This book analyzes these and related developments with a quasi-historical perspective.

Today's urban Texas landscape contains Chicano street and prison gangs, with hybrid offshoots emerging from power struggles within those groups and from the forces of migration and technology. As a place with a balance of old- and new-age community structure, San Antonio provides an ideal setting for a study of these dynamics. It has a large Chicano poor and working-class population; it is highly segregated by race, ethnicity, and social class; it is a popular tourist destination that offers camouflage to outsiders; and it is reasonably high-tech. In terms of its geography, culture, and secondary economy, it is not a border town *per se*, but it is close enough to have a rich Mexican heritage and to be a major distribution corridor for drug cartels.

The barrio criminal networks of today avail themselves of social media, mobile phone technology, increased access to personal vehicles, automatic weapons, and drug contacts in Mexico. I thus address how such social and technological advances have affected barrio networking processes and the intensity of the street lifestyle over time. Intergenerational shifts and the tension that accompanies them are also central themes in the work. With such a long history of barrio gang activity and illegal drug distribution, we can generalize the lessons learned from San Antonio to other urban centers with longstanding Latino populations. How levels of human and social capital bear upon one's position in the barrio network structure as detailed herein are no doubt similar to processes found in other Chicano communities in Texas and the Southwest.

Most of my adult life to date has been spent in San Antonio, where as a young man, I was a street-gang intervention social worker. As a university professor there from 2003 to 2015, I continued to focus on the specific social group some might refer to as the *criminal element*. This work questions whether such a neat categorization of persons exists, and if so, what its parameters may be. Even when studying that segment of poor, street-oriented subjects that most would assume are members of the so-called "underclass," I encountered many unexpected class-based contradictions that shed light on the less-known contours of the barrio criminal underworld. I contend that social class divisions among Chicanos in prior generations may not be as marked as they are today. I find that many members of the so-called criminal class once had access to considerable social and human capital, often blurring the lines between "underclass" and normative socioeconomic standing, behaviors, and networks.

Staying true to the principles of ethnography, this work is in large part a representation of the views, attitudes, and experiences of its primary research subjects, former 1950s barrio gang members now in their late seventies and early eighties. Their collective concerns about the misrepresentation of their subculture in the media and the larger society over time prompted these collaborators to express a strong interest in assuring that I "got it right." I thus sought to capture the many nuances, paradoxes, and other complexities of their time and experience. As a result, this is largely a sociological work on poor and working-class experiences of Mexican American boys in inner-city San Antonio in the 1950s. As it profiles the life trajectories of many members of this generation to include those of their children and grandchildren, the work also addresses contemporary criminological theories on developmental or "life-course" criminology (e.g. Laub and Sampson 2003; Thornberry et al. 2003) and intergenerational transfer of criminal propensity and lifestyle (e.g. Besemer 2012; Farrington 2011).

This study also demonstrates that when one is willing to become fully immersed in the work via embedded ethnography, unanticipated resources open up. Early in the study, a single attempt was made to secure funding from a federal humanities agency, and although it was scored highly, the study was not funded. Due to the aging of my primary research subjects, and the demanding nature of the fieldwork involved to find them and gain their trust, I had little time to continue to seek such funding. I simply pushed forward and let the study assume a life of its own. As a result, I formed closer working friendships with these folks than I had anticipated, intertwining my life's activities with those of my research subjects wherever possible.

From past fieldwork experiences with the gang population, I've concluded that research subjects in this project opened themselves up in ways that they might not have done if they'd received formal stipends for participation in a well-funded project. Instead of handing out a cashier's check for participation and requesting a signature for receipt of payment as is customary in funded studies with bureaucratic paper trails, I was able to offer less formal tokens of appreciation and eventually my friendship in exchange for their participation. This enhanced the level of trust needed to collect information elder subjects deem sensitive, if not sacred, and increased the efficiency of the data gathering.

Chapter Previews

Chapter 1 begins with the musings of an ethnographer who has spent the first twenty years of his academic career studying Chicano gangs in San Antonio, Texas. It offers insights on information flow among street criminals, how reputations are obtained, and how small a social milieu this underworld seems to be. Using theory on criminal propensity and the finite nature of the chronic offender group, I ponder the existence of a criminal subclass that seems to be a permanent feature of society, and more specifically, of the many barrios in San Antonio.

Chapter 1 also details the research project that gave impetus to this book, a qualitative study of the local barrio gangs of the 1940s,'50s, and '60s. The goals, methods, and challenges of the work are detailed here. Finally, a descriptive set of findings estimating the size of the Chicano youth gang population in the 1950s and in the first decade of the 2000s in San Antonio is presented around the criminal-class argument. The implications of these estimates are offered, setting the stage for the book's main thrust on Chicano street-gang networks.

Chapter 2 profiles some of the earliest street-corner delinquent groups to emerge in San Antonio and their ecological contexts. While groups that existed from the 1930s through the 1950s are still revered by certain segments of a past generation, these are not among the most notorious groups in the city's modern gang folklore. This raises several key issues about the structure and continuity of barrio networks addressed throughout the book. The displacement of residents from the city's core due to urban redevelopment, the emergence of government-subsidized housing for low income residents in the 1940s, and other social changes in the urban environment caused street gangs to undergo significant changes in network and organizational structure. An issue addressed here that is not seen in much previous gang literature is whether those original roots have any bearing on barrio processes in the newer locations gangs expanded into in subsequent generations.

Drawing on the estimated size of the barrio street-gang universe, and on data collected in interview and focus-group activities, chapter 3 begins to explore the structure of barrio social networks. The backgrounds, institutional experiences, and adult life trajectories of barrio gang members and their families help to shape the intergenerational network. Several elements not traditionally a part of gang subculture condition its networks as well. Subjects' ties to the military, public service, and other occupations are some of the more surprising elements of the experiences of 1950s barrio-gang youth. Such paradoxical findings evidence normative levels of human and social capital among these gang participants. While the "underclass" framework is often used to characterize today's gang youth, it appears to be less fitting for the 1950s barrio-gang generation.

Chapter 4 addresses some of the important remaining contexts for defining and giving substance to the 1950s barrio gang scene. It speaks to the era's level of delinquent intensity, and profiles the government-subsidized housing projects, popular youth hangouts, and other staging areas near downtown. These are the places where much social posturing, gang fighting, and other reputation-forming events occurred. Chapter 4 also profiles many of the central figures in this atmosphere, going back to the 1940s. I describe how for these well-known members of the subculture, their street gang days often positioned them to excel in their illegitimate business dealings as adult *ruedas* (major players).

Chapter 5 addresses barrio expansion, the explosion of the drug scene in the 1960s and '70s, and the state's incarceration binge. This was known locally as the "Fred Carrasco era." Carrasco was perhaps the best-known barrio boy turned rueda to emerge from San Antonio's slums. His life is chronicled in *The Heroin Merchant* by Wilson McKinney (1975), and in portions of books more recently written by David Montejano (2010), and Ben Olguin (2010). Those works characterize Carrasco as a charismatic, intelligent Chicano who easily could have been successful in legitimate pursuits. He employed many San Antonio barrio youth, a fact that is barely recognized in prior works on his life, but it is common knowledge among the many persons interviewed for this study.

I critique McKinney's (1975) work as a limited perspective of this era's underworld dynamics, often viewed through the lens of the narcotics detectives he shadowed. His work didn't chronicle the barrio connections to fully illustrate the importance of the street to higher-level operations across generations. Chapter 5 therefore builds on the book's timeline to define the network structure that preceded and enabled a character like Carrasco to emerge from the barrio. In the process, it shows how the Carrasco clan influenced the prison gangs of the next generation who would come to dominate the 1980s heroin trade.

Chapter 6 details the emergence of Chicano prison gangs in Texas in the 1980s. Taking their cue from the Carrasco-era clans, these groups begin terrorizing the barrios and menacing the street gangs to cooperate or face consequences. The chapter covers "blood in" initiations, swearing oaths, collecting taxes from non-gang dealers, groups killing their own for transgressions against the group, and the targeting of competitors for violence. There is war with rival prison gangs of other races and bloody battles between Latino prison gangs. Chapter 6 cuts across several decades to address generational friction. It depicts how the Latino prison gangs of the 1980s and 1990s relate to the older (pre-1960s) and younger generations. The latest of the younger groups are called Tangos, street-to-prison hybrids that emerged in San Antonio and other Texas cities in full force in the early 2000s. This chapter addresses the cultural similarities and differences in Chicano barrio-gang norms across several generations.

Chapter 7 examines the delinquent peer group in Chicano barrios with a broad historical lens by profiling its most recent developments. It further explores questions raised in previous chapters regarding how modern groups compare to their predecessors. An impetus for this chapter, and for the work as a whole, is whether the etiology and other features of the modern Chicano barrio gang resemble the archetypal local street-corner phenomenon where boyhood playgroups evolve to more insidious ones. What is the role of modernity and technology in altering the traditional rumor mill, gang recruitment processes, and the multi-generational network structure depicted throughout the book? Might one expect to find substantial network links across the generations, for example? I draw on the modern gang literature, on my own cumulative knowledge of this subculture, and that of expert gang investigators working in San Antonio to answer these questions. Finally, a closing chapter 8 summarizes the study's major findings, assessing the lessons learned about permanency and change in the Chicano barrio gangs over time.

One

Is There Such a Thing as the Criminal Class?

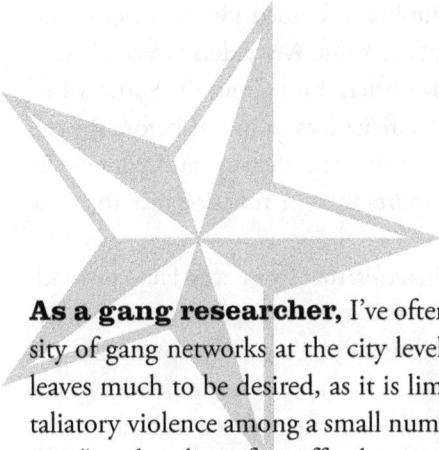

As a gang researcher, I've often wondered about the size and density of gang networks at the city level. So far, the research on this topic leaves much to be desired, as it is limited to work on predatory and retaliatory violence among a small number of gangs (Hughes 2013; Vargas 2014) and on lists of co-offenders in official arrest reports (Pappachristos 2013). In my fieldwork, I have noticed that those most entrenched in the criminal lifestyle often have widespread reputations—at a minimum, among other offenders and the police. This is so even in a large city like San Antonio, and even in a modern era where the size of the gang population would seem to be too large for this to occur. To better appreciate this possibility, one must first consider that most juvenile delinquents do not continue engaging in crime as adults (Piquero and Brezina 2001), and that even most adult criminals desist their illegal activities by middle age (Laub and Sampson 2003). Second, it is well-known that only about 6 to 8 percent of all male arrestees in a given population will continue on a path to become chronic offenders (Wolfang, Thornberry, and Figlio 1987). Therefore, this leaves a relatively small group of notable offenders (i.e., true outlaws) whose legacies may carry on among the poor and working classes especially, depending on the types of crimes they have committed and the groups they may have belonged to.

Another observation I've made in the field is that many gang members seem to obtain surprisingly accurate information about significant events involving other known criminals rather quickly and efficiently. They often have key information about unsolved crimes and are aware of victimizations that aren't known to the police and arrests that are not publicized in the media. Young gang members tend to recount narratives they've heard regarding worthy events and people in the barrio, and these tales can eventually become a form of urban folklore. These facets of barrio life led me to wonder about the nature of the rumor mill, how it worked, and what the roles of families, extended kin, and fictive kin were in the transmission of such information. My elderly research subjects spoke of the *alambre* (wire) that existed throughout the barrio when they were in their prime. That it was efficient, even in eras before the cell phone and social media, suggests that the size, density, and parameters of the network are perhaps more important to its functionality than the medium of transmission.

The idea that there exists a criminal *class* that forms a de facto network within which barrio information is spread invokes a well-known theoretical tenet about the prevalence of criminality in a given population. It is generally agreed that there is some small segment of any population that is most likely to engage in crime, i.e. who are, through some combination of nature and nurture, prone to deviance, aggression, etc. Some would say this is the segment of the population that possesses the traits of low self-control (see Gottfredson & Hirschi 1990 for a description of these traits or Burt et al. 2014 for recent work on this topic). While low self-control is thought to be present in some small population segment of every society, it is not well agreed upon whether it is an inborn (nature) or learned (nurture) set of characteristics. Although the concept is a bit over-simplified here, it is a useful way to begin thinking about the characteristics of those who might belong to the barrio's street-information network. Who are the people with the dubious distinction of being part of the "criminal element" in this context and why are they part of it?

To begin addressing this issue, I suggest that gang membership is a good proxy for estimating the size and scope of the most crime-prone subgroup or those who truly belong to the so-called criminal element in a given population. While this is certainly not without weaknesses as an estimate, and contrary to other cogent conceptualizations of gangs *not* being synonymous with crime (e.g. Duran 2012), one could do much worse. For example, using arrest records to identify "criminals" turns problematic in that there are otherwise upstanding citizens with multiple DUI arrests, or public protesters with rap sheets for disorderly conduct, which seems to miss the mark for the "criminal element." In the other direction, some (albeit few) adept criminals have never or seldom been arrested.[1]

A host of other facts support the use of gang membership as a proxy for the criminal class. For most academics, law enforcement practitioners, and the general public alike, gang involvement is nearly synonymous with a delinquent lifestyle. Let us also consider that the gang literature estimates the proportion of the nation's youth population that is gang involved at a mere 2 to 5 percent (Greene and Pranis 2007; Pyrooz & Sweeten 2015; Tapia 2011), which is similar to the proportion of the population that are chronic offenders. In smaller geographic areas, the gang prevalence estimates range more widely, from 5 to 25 percent, depending on place and era (Hughes 2005). The upper ranges are estimated for high-poverty areas (Howell 2001), which characterizes the social-class position of a large segment of the Chicano community in San Antonio.

It is worth noting that half of all gang members in the United States are said to be Latinos (Green and Pranis 2007; Rosenthal 2000). So in the Chicano community, we might expect the proportion of gang-involved youth to fall on the high end of the range seen in the literature. The US Chicano population is a poor ethnic group comprising the largest segment of Latinos, and the socioeconomic status of this group has not improved much, either in Texas (Murdock et al. 2013) or the nation (Grogger and Trejo 2002). To think about the criminal subclass in this group, it is important to know the proportion that is gang involved. To arrive there, this chapter provides some background for the current study and an estimate of the size of San Antonio's barrio youth gang population in the mid 1950s and in the early 2000s for comparison.

Going Back in Time

The research project that gave impetus to this book was a data collection effort gathered from a sample of elderly men who were gang members in San Antonio in their teens. Having lived in various low-income San Antonio barrios since the early 1990s, and intermingling with the gang population through past occupations and other forms of social interaction, I'd heard many stories of the infamous gangs of the 1950s.[2] The reputations and urban legends associated with many 1950s barrio groups and their members are essentially common knowledge among the large working-class population in San Antonio, but few academics have documented this aspect of the city's social history. In terms of published work, only David Montejano (2010) has ventured into this terrain in the early chapters of his much broader view of Chicano political movements in San Antonio, but even there, the focus was on the late 1950s and early 1960s.[3]

I wanted to explore the Chicano street-gang phenomenon in that city as far back as possible, and I began a study of barrio gangs of the 1950s. The most basic goal was to preserve the history of what many believed to be an old-fashioned, less intense era of gang activity than we have today, for a general comparison of norms and structure. There was a reasonable sample of surviving gang members from that era, but in most cases they were quite elderly. The race was on to reach them and build enough trust and rapport to be able to tell their stories before these individuals died. Subconsciously, I may have also considered such a study to be a public service to San Antonio's poor and working-class communities—a way to pay homage to a bygone era of social resistance to ethnic discrimination.[4] Finally, given my longstanding interest in the idea of a criminal subclass, I had a lofty social-science goal of describing the network structure of Chicano gangs over time. Considering that the absolute size of the young male Chicano population in San Antonio in the 1950s was less than one-third of what it is today, and that there was still a large enough group of men alive who could offer information on that era, it was an opportunity to gain some valuable insights on the barrio's network composition.

The work was designed to yield a complete list of the barrio groups that existed citywide, documenting their social origins, their approximate turf boundaries, and other characteristics. A basic objective was to estimate the size of the Chicano male "underclass" (i.e., barrio youth) by determining the number of gangs and the approximate size of each one. The broader study would explore the organizational structure and other subcultural characteristics of these early groups for comparison to those of modern-day Chicano gangs in San Antonio, whom this author has also studied extensively.[5]

The 1950s Barrio Gang Project

Surviving members of the 1950s barrio gangs are a small and hard-to-locate group, ranging in age from their mid-seventies to their mid-eighties.[6] Several subjects have passed away since taking part in the study, which began in the summer of 2012. Unfortunately, several reputable individuals who were still alive when the research began passed away before they could be recruited into the study and interviewed. The thirty-three subjects formally recruited were all reputable former gang members who were "vouched for" by various segments of the community, but namely by each other. As most of the 1950s barrio gang population are deceased, the study relies on subject-provided lists of gangs from throughout the city, and the size of each group is approximated.

Materials collected from the men included hand-drawn maps of neighborhoods with demarcated turf boundaries, old photos, obituaries, miscellaneous materials such as military and prison documents, and even a presidential certificate of clemency for an ex-felon. Subjects also helped to guide the newspaper archive searches conducted for the study, providing names and dates that helped me find key information. The fieldwork continued for three consecutive years, as intensely as time permitted between my other professional duties as a full-time faculty member of the University of Texas at San Antonio. The window of opportunity to conduct the study was small. The aging of surviving participants and first-hand observers of that era made an extensive pursuit of research funding too time-consuming to consider.

The primary method of data collection for this study was face-to-face interviews. Subjects were recruited with snowball sampling, mainly by a word-of-mouth referral system with some screening to authenticate the claim that an individual was a gang member in the 1950s.[7] With the subject's permission, structured interviews were audiotaped. If interviewees preferred not to be recorded, various forms of data, including written responses to a questionnaire, were collected on paper. Throughout the research, I shared my ongoing compilation of information with the subjects, to review and correct or add to regarding their own gangs and rival and neutral gangs, as well as *pintos* (ex-cons) and others who were *mentados* (reputable) in the 1950s street scene in San Antonio (see Appendix C for a glossary of terms).

Unstructured and semi-structured focus group discussions were also a big part of the fieldwork, as many of the surviving members are friends or acquaintances. This was even the case for most of the men who were from rival gangs, and who can now laugh and swap stories together. There were several exceptions, however. There were a few cases involving the surviving siblings of murder victims and other intense rivalries that did not allow for the subjects to interact freely or comfortably, even after nearly sixty years had passed.

Like other contemporary histories of Latino populations (Flippen and Parrado 2012), the project relied heavily on the active participation of subjects as recruiters and as experts on the topic. A core group of about ten subject-collaborators helped to determine other potential subjects' claims of authenticity and to scrutinize information unearthed in the course of the research. Items in the questionnaire used for structured interviews probed subjects' knowledge of which Chicano gangs predominated in the 1940s and 1950s, what their origins and geographical boundaries were, what processes gave rise to their formation, and what contemporary groups may have evolved from these older groups.

Group meetings took place in retirement homes, in cafés, diners, bars, and most importantly, while driving around downtown and the old neighborhoods. On a regular basis, the author drove different small groups of men around various parts of the city, and it brought back many memories for them involving long-gone places, groups, and individuals. It often led to impromptu discussions about the barrio landscape back then, as old rumors were rehashed and past occurrences revisited and retold. As familial, gang, and other barrio network linkages were often explained to me by the men on these excursions, this was one of the most effective and valuable fieldwork strategies in generating data for the study.

Size and Scope Estimation

The counting of gangs and gang members is an inexact and controversial practice in criminology (Ball and Decker 1995; Curry and Decker 1997; Esbensen et al. 2001). Police-generated gang databases in particular are considered to be error-prone for a number of reasons discussed at length in chapter 7 (see also, Jacobs 2009). Still, counting gang members in a given place is not a futile practice. When care is taken to triangulate data sources and to use rigorous methods, reliable estimates can be obtained. As a first step toward understanding the structure of the barrio street scene, I sought to estimate the proportion of Chicano youth in San Antonio that was gang-involved in the 1950s. Then, to gain additional insight on changes over time, namely on the relative size of this group as the San Antonio population grew, I estimated the proportion that was gang-involved in a recent year for comparison.

The total size of the Chicano gang population from the 1950s era was estimated at about 1,200 to 1,300 young men across approximately sixty gangs citywide.[8] This figure was inferred from the approximated size of each of the city's gangs offered by subjects, sizes that ranged from about ten to eighty-five members in each gang, but averaging about twenty members per gang. It was not possible to obtain the names of all individuals in this population universe. Indeed, this exercise served to gauge the feasibility of obtaining a complete inventory of the relevant actors in this era's delinquent subculture, which at the outset seemed plausible, since the Chicano community and its delinquent subset was much smaller back then. Since data collection mainly targeted the central, west, and near-south areas of the city, lists of member names from the far southern, eastern, and northern sectors remained incomplete.

In total, about 475 individuals were named by my sources as having belonged to the inner-city gang subculture throughout the decade of the 1950s. This figure is approximated because of several uncertainties in the data regarding whether some individuals are named more than once. Slight variations in the spelling of names in different subject lists, issues with subject recall, differences in phonetic utterances of names provided by different subjects, and the use of various nicknames by individuals created this issue. There is also a large subset of persons who associated with more than one barrio group, either through residence relocation or other circumstances (discussed further in chapter 3), which created some uncertainty over whether the same person shows up in more than one group. Some nicknames used are also very common to the US Chicano gang subculture in general, such as the five "Jokers" /Joka/, the three "Killers" /Kila/, and the six *Borrados* named here.[9] Despite diligent attempts to clarify, some of these issues were never fully resolved. The list of approximately 475 individuals' names compiled in this study represents about 35 percent of the total barrio-youth street-gang member universe.

It was ultimately unrealistic to expect that all 1950s barrio gang members could be named in the research. Although it is a finite underclass population, i.e., a loose network of gang members, drug users, petty criminals, and other barrio dwellers, many of whom knew each other personally or at least by reputation, it had been fifty-five to sixty years since the targeted time period had passed. Not having the time to find, reach, build rapport, etc. with representatives of all sixty gangs also made the task impractical for the lone ethnographer. Furthermore, while the authenticity and accuracy of oral history is still debated (Batty 2009; Oelofse 2011), the limitations of the method in the current research context are clear. The degradation of memory that is thought to accompany the aging process was one of the primary threats to validity (Brickman and Stern 2009). However, I relied on *saturation* as a fieldwork method; that is, once a social fact was reiterated enough times, it was confirmed as valid. Therefore, these approximately 475 names collected were perhaps the most reputable individuals in the inner-city barrio subculture of the era.

What Percentage of Chicano Youth Is Gang Involved?

1950s Estimate

To estimate the proportion of young Chicanos in the general population belonging to the barrio gang subculture, the total estimated number of gang members is set to the appropriate population base. Informed by the age of onset in interview data, by the literature on typical age ranges among American street gangs (Klein 1995; Spergel, Wa, and Sosa 2005), and by the conceptual parameters of the study to address "youth gangs" *per se*, an age range of twelve to nineteen is used as the base. Although census data on Hispanics did not exist until 1970 (Cohn 2010), one can extrapolate rough estimates for an earlier period by working backward from existing census data on Hispanics.

To illustrate, Current Population Survey data for the year 2000 shows about 54,500 Hispanic males in San Antonio ages twelve to nineteen (US Census Bureau, 2014). Roughly 10 percent of these Hispanics were of a national origin "other than Mexican" i.e., non-Chicano, leaving about 49,500 as the base, or 4.3 percent of the total population of San Antonio. Doing this operation for 1990 shows this group of male Chicano teens to represent about 3.7 percent of the city's population, and moving backward to 1970, this group represents about 3.3 percent of the total population. At this rate, placing young Chicano males at 3 percent of the total 1950 San Antonio population (500,460), one derives a base of about 15,000 Chicano males ages twelve to nineteen. My estimate of 1,200 to 1,300 Chicano gang members in that era thus represents about 8.5 percent of the Chicano youth population.

Given the validity issues the literature identifies with the quality of police-generated gang databases, this method is at least as good, if not better than a modern estimate using police data. The authentication and saturation processes involved in the 1950s estimate are among the most rigorous of methods used for generating reliable lists of members in qualitative gang fieldwork, and is not commonly seen in other studies. Although it is a rough estimate, it is worth comparing to a modern estimate obtained with police data, which as stated, has its own flaws, but undoubtedly includes many of the same types of chronic offenders in a given era that a peer nomination process would.

2007 Estimate

Since the absolute size of the male Chicano population ages twelve to nineteen in San Antonio has more than tripled since the 1950s, the method used to estimate the number of gang youth for that era was not viable for generating a modern estimate. The only count of gang members by race and ethnicity for San Antonio is maintained by the police. The San Antonio Police Department (SAPD) gang data from 2007 showed 6,535 male, Latino gang members in the "active" database.[10] Management of this database is governed by a limited timeframe for inclusion of any member.[11] This count also includes roughly 1,500 members of adult Latino prison and motorcycle gangs. When deducted from the current count, this yields an estimate of about 5,000 street-gang-involved Chicano youth in 2007. Current Population Survey data from 2007 shows about 51,300 Mexican-origin Hispanic males ages twelve to nineteen in San Antonio (US Census Bureau 2014). The rough estimate of the proportion of young Chicano males in San Antonio that was gang involved in 2007 is thus just under 10 percent, slightly higher than the 8.5 percent estimated for the 1950s era, yet remarkably comparable, given the distance between the two points in time.

Size Estimate Implications

That the proportion of Chicano youth that is gang involved is so similar in two distinct and far-apart eras in San Antonio has a profound implication for the criminal class framework. Where the estimates were obtained using different methodologies and still wound up remarkably similar speaks to the consistency of the relative size of the criminal class.[12] It hardly seems likely that this result is pure coincidence or due to differences in methodology, as both police and gang members themselves tend to have a good sense of who is truly gang involved. Rather it appears to support the theoretical principles about the size of the most crime-prone segment of the population found in the literature on chronic offenders discussed earlier in this chapter.

Given this basic finding, the next chapter begins to add substance to the portrayal of the social milieu of the early San Antonio barrio gangster. It includes a description of the origins of these groups in the once-vibrant red-light district in the city's inner West Side. This context, coupled with the typical Chicano youths' social position as a poor, segregated, ethnic minority with few opportunity structures, paved the way for a barrio street culture to take root and thrive for decades to come. I profile some of the city's original barrio street gangs, which served as predecessors to future groups that would morph in the face of social change over the years.

Two

Barrio Group Origins: Micro-locality and Community

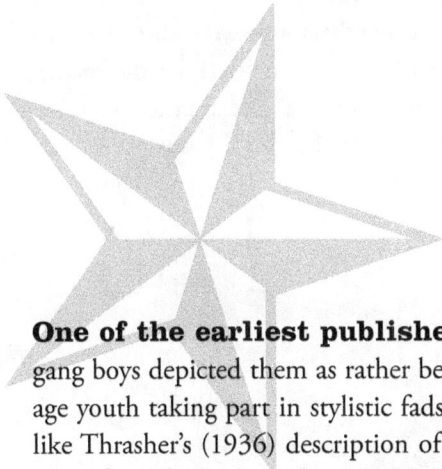

One of the earliest published works on Mexican American gang boys depicted them as rather benign groups, if not simply as average youth taking part in stylistic fads (Bogardus 1943). This was much like Thrasher's (1936) description of Chicago street gangs as an evolution of poorly supervised street-corner playgroups. Bogardus considered these group formations to have emerged out of social class divisions and language barriers, creating a subclass of poverty-stricken misfits out for mischief and excitement when banded together. Later, Mirandé (1987), Vigil (1988), and Montejano (2010) would offer similar versions of this to describe the emergence of barrio gangs as a form of social resistance or counterculture in the face of discrimination.

Accounts of early forms of barrio "gangs," or groups of boys who congregated on San Antonio's inner city street corners, mostly conformed to the academic depiction. An account of such a group from the 1930s comes from an archived audiotape of a barrio boy turned prominent municipal and county official. In an "early life" oral history interview, Albert Peña, a teen in the 1930s, described the Riverside gang on the northwestern edge of downtown near Fox Tech High School.

> The group started out as an athletic club who played against neighboring barrio groups like the boys from the Moonglow and Irving Jr. High [The Espiga gang]....we loitered in the later hours, protected our neighborhood, held parties, drank home brew, and stole items off of delivery trucks when we could. Sometimes the sandlot ballgames with the other

barrios led to disputes, and if it couldn't be settled, it led to gang fights or selected one-on-one fights. (UTSA 1996).

By 1950, Riverside and Espiga were among the most notorious groups in the city. A newspaper article from that year described the disciplinary measures used by these groups against members who were disloyal to the gang as especially harsh. While perhaps sensationalized for the media, juvenile officers stated that snitches were given a special tattoo marking between the eyes and that a second incident of disloyalty was punishable by death (*San Antonio Light* 1950).

Shoeshine Boy, San Antonio, Texas, 1949. *Russell Lee Photograph Collection, Center for American History, University of Texas at Austin.*

The Shoeshine Scene

One of the early manifestations of Chicano street-youth cliques was the groups who congregated at various shoeshine stands in the down-town-west area (Casillas 1994). Many of these youth carried around their own makeshift shoeshine boxes and peddled illicit shines, as this practice was prohibited in the downtown area by city ordinance (City of San Antonio 1940). One of the old sayings *"boliar de cajon"* is "hustle with the box." While the Chicano context is a bit different in character from that of Irish or Italian street youth, this imagery is similar to depictions of those youth gangs found milling about eastern and midwestern big-city street corners in the early twentieth century (Thrasher 1936; Whyte 1943).

Shoeless youth peddling shines in downtown San Antonio, ca. 1950. *Courtesy of the personal photo collection of Juan "Chota" Mendoza.*

Kid with his shoeshine box, San Antonio, ca. 1950. *Courtesy of the personal photo collection of Juan "Chota" Mendoza.*

As a common barrio entrepreneurial practice in this era, peddling the shoeshine is culturally relevant for San Antonio Chicanos, as reflected in the still-popular saying "*dále shine.*" It now roughly translates as "go for it" or "give it a shot." Some of the main downtown hangouts for early street-corner groups were *Tony's Mirror Shine* and the *Alameda Shoeshine Stand*, both on Houston Street. That the mobile shoeshine boy was prohibited from doing business in public streets by law but was still part of the "hustle" of early delinquent groups also speaks to the ethnic-based social resistance aspect of early Chicano gangs (Bogardus 1942; Mirandé 1987; Montejano 2012; Vigil 1988), and West Side San Antonio subcultures specifically (Marquez et al. 2007).

Stands further to the west of downtown such as the Especial and the Red-Light had jukeboxes and billiards tables, attracting area youth to congregate and smoke cigarettes, marijuana, etc. West Side shoeshine stands were therefore perceived by the public as having a bit of a rougher quality and were the preferred hangouts for barrio youth.

In early academic literature on the settlement of San Antonio, the West Side was characterized as the "outstanding slum area . . . of unsightly congested dwellings and commercialized vice" (Chambers 1940: 298).

Even today, "the West Side" is a commonly used phrase with various meanings to include quintessential barrio conditions, Mexican heritage, folkways, pride; and for some, it has a slightly pejorative connotation to suggest lower-class attitudes or behaviors. A common utterance heard among native San Antonio Hispanics, for those to whom it applies, is to claim "West Side" or "*soy del West Side,*" which speaks volumes to most locals. It connotes that the claimant is likely street savvy, has seen or experienced poverty on a firsthand basis, and is someone not to be "messed with." It is therefore intuitive that this is where the barrio youth gang phenomenon emerged most robustly in San Antonio.

Los Bounds/El West Side Bounds

The western edge of modern-day downtown San Antonio was once known as the red-light district, a.k.a. "the Bounds," or for some Chicanos, "*El Rejuego*" (playzone). Judging from newspaper archives from over a century ago, this is where some of the first street-corner barrio youth groups and crime rings existed as well (*San Antonio Light*, 1910; 1914). The groups from that area documented in 1950s local newsprint were tied to now-extinct alleyways and street corners in the West Side core that were adjacent to and part of the city's red-light district. The area was redeveloped by freeway construction and other economic development in west downtown in the early 1960s, wiping away neighborhoods and displacing its residents to other parts of the city.

Several of these early groups' hangouts were situated in what is now the popular tourist area *Market Square* and the downtown campus of the University of Texas at San Antonio (see Figure 1 below). In the 1940s and 1950s barrio gang youth knew this part of town as El Bounds, or Los Bounds. A variant is "El West Side Bounds," as seen in the graffiti scrawled in the 1957 photo below taken from the *San Antonio Express* Newspaper photo archives at UTSA's Institute of Texan Cultures.

The Bounds of the 1950s was essentially San Antonio's original red-light district going back at least to the 1880s, judging from the reform movement to officially license and regulate brothels in 1889 by

Juvenile Bureau Det. Sgt. Leonard "Toto" Salas inspects graffiti scribbled on a wall by members of the *West Side Bounds* and the group known as *Los Courts* from the *Alazan Apache* government housing project in the inner West Side. *Courtesy* San Antonio Express *Newspaper photo archives at UTSA's Institute of Texan Cultures.*

city ordinance (Bowser 2003). One eighty-seven-year-old interviewee in this study spoke of the well-known Red Rock bar on the corner of Conchos Street and Matamoros Alley in the Bounds, and who spoke of an active, dangerous area of vice in the late 1940s. For this reason, the area was off limits to soldiers stationed in San Antonio during the first and second world wars (McKinney 1975).

1940s and 1950s Barrio Gangs in the Bounds

Two groups that adopted names most clearly associated with "the district" were the Red Light gang and the West Side Bounds. The Red Light gang most likely took its name from the *Red Light Shoe-Stand*, but much like their 1910s-era predecessors, these boys had various hustles around the west downtown area, and were perhaps considered more of a roaming band of youth than a territorial or turf gang. Research subjects described members of this group as "older guys," meaning they were active since at least the 1940s. Specific names were provided for many of these members, suggesting they were well-known barrio dwellers into the 1950s and beyond (select individuals are profiled in chapter 4). Similarly, boys

The Red Rock Bar. *Courtesy of the personal photo collection of Juan "Chota" Mendoza of San Antonio.*

Below are two pages from San Antonio's infamous *Blue Book*. First circulated in 1910, it was a guide to speakeasies, brothels, and the like located in "The District" (i.e. The Bounds). Bowser (2003) identified ninety-one separate locations within the roughly one square mile of the district where one could partake in the activities uniquely offered there. The majority of these were listed in the *Blue Book. Author's collection.*

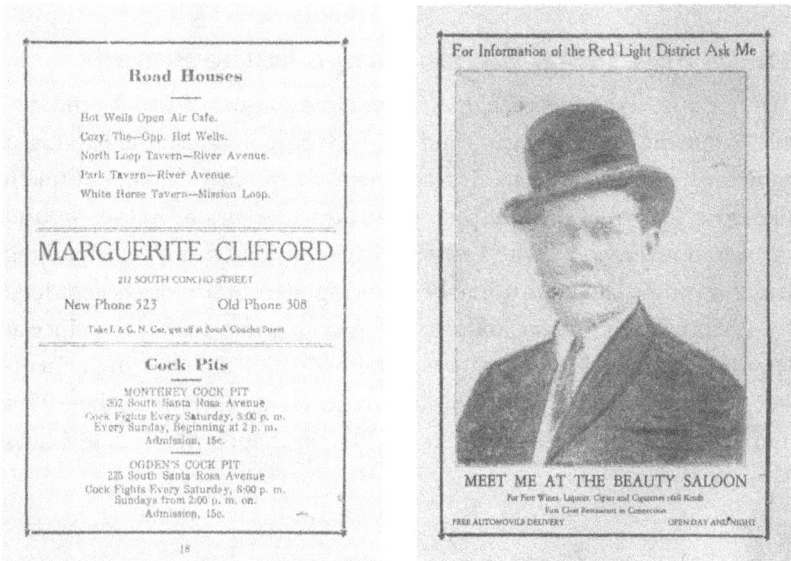

Road Houses

Hot Wells Open Air Cafe.
Cozy, The—Opp. Hot Wells.
North Loop Tavern—River Avenue.
Park Tavern—River Avenue.
White Horse Tavern—Mission Loop.

MARGUERITE CLIFFORD

212 SOUTH CONCHO STREET

New Phone 523   Old Phone 308

Take I. & G. N. Car, get off at South Concho Street

Cock Pits

MONTEREY COCK PIT
312 South Santa Rosa Avenue
Cock Fights Every Saturday, 8:00 p. m.
Every Sunday, Beginning at 2 p. m.
Admission, 15c.

OGDEN'S COCK PIT
235 South Santa Rosa Avenue
Cock Fights Every Saturday, 8:00 p. m. on.
Sundays from 2:00 p. m. on.
Admission, 15c.

For Information of the Red Light District Ask Me

MEET ME AT THE BEAUTY SALOON
For Fine Wines, Liquors, Cigars and Cigarettes of all Kinds
Fine Class Restaurant in Connection
FREE AUTOMOBILE DELIVERY   OPEN DAY AND NIGHT

from the West Side Bounds may not have had a specific claim to turf, as the Bounds was a large vicinity. Aside from committing petty crimes and peddling shoeshines and newspapers, there were various ways for barrio boys to make money in the downtown area, such as an activity they called the "throw-penny." It consisted of groups of boys descending to congregate on the banks of the San Antonio River by Soledad and Commerce Street to call out to military GIs walking by on the street level to toss pennies down to them. Interviewees described how the boys would often turn to taunting the GIs, causing them to hurl quarters at the boys in an effort to teach them a lesson. The boys would dodge the projectiles and then dive down into the shallow river to recover them.

La Paloma, Los Cocos, Las Americas, Los Gallos, El Wesley (pictured below), and the Boys Club were the other barrio street gangs that were most active in the Bounds in the 1940s and 1950s.

69. BOYS FROM THE BARRIOS - WESLEY
HOUSE ON LEONA / COLIMA ST

El Wesley street gang. *Courtesy of the personal photo collection of Teodoro "Lolo" Gonzales of San Antonio.*

The next sections detail what was learned about these and other inner-city groups in this research. True to a notion of "community" that some argue has been lost in a large, modern society growing in complexity and anonymity (Putnam 2000), the commonality among these groups was their hyper-local nature. "Back then there was a little *clikita* every two to three street corners claiming their turf and willing to fight for pride and respect" ("Juan Chota," Los Cocos). "Back then, *la raza* was more unified, it was a much smaller world, a community with the barber, the corner store, etc., everyone knew everyone, you'd see them everywhere" ("Lefty," Los Courts).

Barrio La Paloma

Aside from the more nomadic groups referenced above, Barrio La Paloma is one of the earliest documented residential area groups of Chicano street-corner youth with a specific barrio name discovered in this study.[13] The group was associated with Paloma Alley, one of the oldest alleyways in San Antonio (*San Antonio Light*, 1949). In the 1920s, this area housed Mexican midwives and their families, several of whom kept a flock of white pigeons and doves in the yard—hence La Paloma. The group was documented in an early 1940s *corrido* by a popular Mexican artist of the era, Jose Morante, in *"Los Chavos de la Paloma."* The protagonist sings about first arriving in San Antonio as a destitute stranger looking for excitement and being taken in by a band of streetwise youth from La Paloma.

Most participants in this study recalled the presence of this gang, but there were no known surviving members to interview. Any survivors of the last cohort of members of this gang would now be in their late eighties. A mid-1950s member of one of the gangs adjacent to Barrio La Paloma recalled the names of several members, and these were included on the list for that group. A member of a well-known West Side family known as los Italianos who ran a bar in the Bounds in the 1940s and 1950s recalled a pair of brothers known as *Los Camarones* (the Shrimp) who were members of La Paloma, and whose family subsequently moved to Chicago.[14] Not much more is known about this early group, who were likely one of San Antonio's very first *residential area* barrio street-corner youth gangs from the Bounds.

Los Cocos

Another of the groups from the Bounds, known for being one of the tougher groups around and made somewhat notorious by the local press in a high-profile rape case in 1951, was the group associated with *Los Cocos* bakery on the corner of Guadalupe and Laredo Streets in modern-day west downtown. This was a classical age-graded Chicano *klika* (see Moore 1978; Vigil 1988), with older and younger subgroups that age in and out of the gang. It is not known when the group formed, but it dissipated with urban redevelopment in the early 1960s.

According to two of its surviving members, Juan "Chota" and "El Dracula," at any given time this group had about twenty to twenty-five active members. An example of how the urban lore of such a group lived on in exaggerated fashion, a news article in the *San Antonio Light* on barrio gang history erroneously placed the group at over one hundred members (Rosales 1987). The episode that brought them some notoriety in 1951

Los Cocos Bakery. *Courtesy of Luciano Benavidez of San Antonio.*

Los Cocos Gang. *Courtesy of the personal collection of Vidal "El Panther" Rendon.*

involved five of its *calotes* (older cohort), one of whom was arrested for the rape of a woman at gunpoint. Three other members engaged in witness intimidation against a fifth member who ultimately perjured himself on the stand to avoid testifying against the defendant in court (*San Antonio Express-News* 1951(a)). Contrary to common notions about the nonseriousness of 1950s street gangs, such stories suggest that they could be quite antisocial. This is an issue of constant debate among various segments of the Chicano community who provided insights for this study, including social workers and police of the era, and especially among 1950s and 1960s gangsters. The era in which the gang phenomenon was most intense and lethal is a subject I return to in chapter 3 and at other points in the book.

Other Groups from the Bounds

Adjacent to Los Cocos turf was the group associated with Las Americas bakery. Their street corner was Conchos and Matamoros, in the heart of the red-light district. It was near the infamous Red Rock bar where various brothels—known in the early 1900s as "cribs"—formerly stood (Bowser 2003; Sanders 2014). *Las Americas* was said to be a small group compared to other known groups in the area. Nonetheless, like Los Cocos, this group received some notoriety in local press coverage of their violent crimes (*San Antonio Express-News* 1955).

Another group from the area was Los Gallos, which was also a bakery and store that served as a hangout for boys from surrounding streets and alleys. One of the larger groups from the Bounds was the group associated with the Boys Club No. 1 (current west downtown). It too was an age-graded group with *calotes* and *chavalones*, with some eighty members in total throughout the 1950s ("Blackie," The Boys Club). It stood on the now-extinct Matamoros Alley between Frio and Leona Streets, where a Doubletree Hotel now sits across from the UT San Antonio Downtown Campus (see Figure 1 below). This community recreation center was a popular hangout with numerous resources. It had a library, a craft-making shop, Ping-Pong and billiards tables, a television set, checkers and chess sets, a boxing gym in the basement, a baseball field, basketball courts, and a swimming pool. It thus drew a large number of area youth.[15]

The Wesley Community Center is one of San Antonio's oldest comprehensive social service providers to the barrio. Located in the heart of the Bounds on Colima Street from 1917 to 1970, this Methodist-founded agency was a dynamic and nationally accredited settlement house with numerous educational, wellness, and betterment programs (*San Antonio Express-News* 1950). Like the Boys Club, and similar other centers such as the West Side's House of Neighborly Services, there was a large juvenile barrio gang associated with it. The Wesley House grew to three centers by 1953, one of which was the Riverside Community House, to which the Riverside gang corresponded in the 1950s. In the early 1960s, the Wesley Center established its future home in the Columbia Heights area in the deep South Side, a poor, blighted area with social conditions similar to those of the West Side.

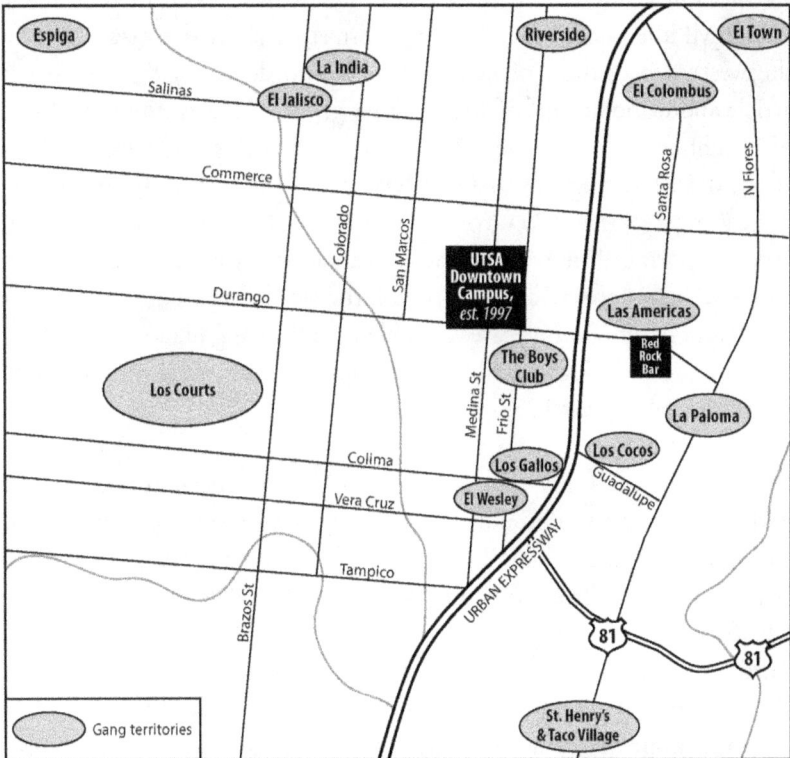

Figure 1: The Bounds (right of expressway) and Inner West Side (left of expressway) showing 1950s gang turfs. *Map by Isabelle Burke.*

As shown in Figure 1, on the northern edge of the Bounds were El Columbus, the aforementioned Riverside [Cats], El Town, and to the northwest edge, Espiga. El Columbus was a group of about twenty to twenty-five members associated with Columbus Park and the Knights of Columbus Catholic Church. Their turf is marked by Columbus Street on the map above, but it extended to the Santa Rosa hospital area by Martin Street and the Expressway north of Market Square. Riverside was a neighborhood adjacent to San Pedro Creek between Columbus and *El Town*, by Martin Street and North Flores.[16] The Saints was a group associated with St. Henry's parish just south of downtown, and the adjacent group to the south was Taco Village, named after the café where the group hung out.

El Espiga, one of the oldest West Side gangs, was centered on the Irving Middle School on Zarzamora Street (just off the map above to the west), where most of its members attended. In a 1953 newspaper article about the decline of street-corner gangs in San Antonio, a House of Neighborly Services youth worker referred to this "old gang" as "just about dead," stating the challenge was now to keep kids from reviving these groups (*San Antonio Express-News* 1953). It does not seem to be an accurate portrayal, however, as around that same time its members still appeared before the juvenile court with the word *Espiga* tattooed on their hands and bodies. In one case, a female with the gang name on her cheek went before the judge refusing to explain the tattoo's significance (*San Antonio Express-News* 1952-a).

Although the inner East Side has traditionally been considered the African American community in San Antonio, there were pockets of Mexican and Chicano families there in the 1950s as well. One vicinity was commonly referred to as the East End in the 1950s, and the primary East Side Chicano gang was known as *Los Vatos de La calle* Austin (the Austin Street gang). Farther to the north were the guys from La Piedrera, also known as the Rock Quarry (RQs), as most of these families worked in San Antonio's rock mining industry in that area.[17] In an adjacent residential area, along the main commercial artery of San Pedro Avenue (just off the map below), was Varrio Kenwood, named after a small park in the area. This was not a traditional settlement area for Chicanos in the

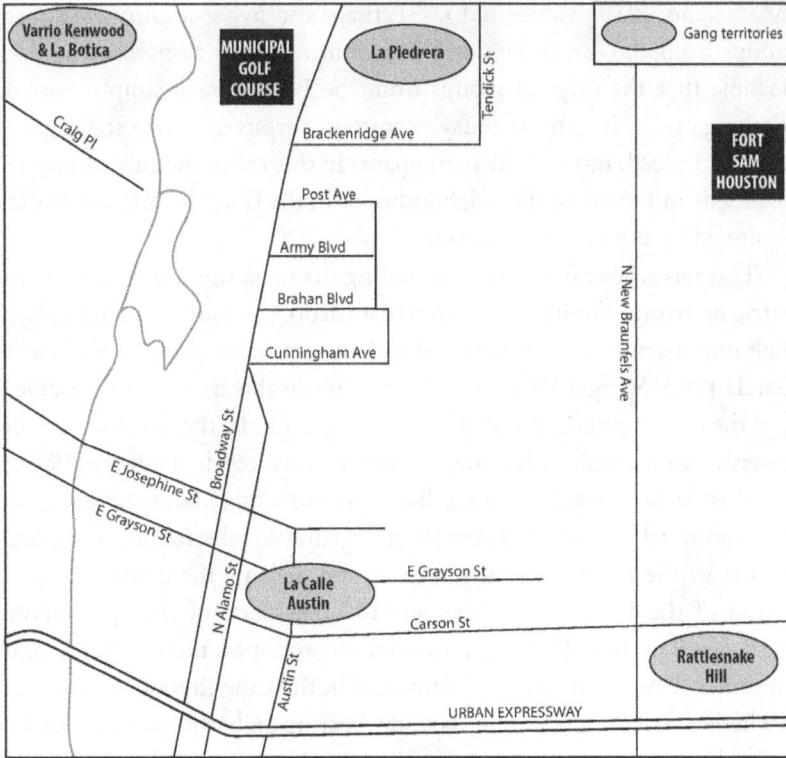

Figure 2: North East inner city showing 1950s gang turfs.
Map by Isabelle Burke.

1950s, and this gang was a mixed-race group of the children of black and Mexican domestic workers employed by more affluent white families to the north of downtown ("El Calvo," Varrio Kenwood).

Changes in the Barrio Landscape

The ecological contexts of some of the earliest known barrio street-corner delinquent groups to emerge in San Antonio would be disrupted in the late 1950s. While the 1930s through early 1950s groups are still revered by certain segments of a past generation, very few of them are part of the city's current barrio gang folklore. Those with the most notoriety today were very large groups that emerged in neighborhoods several miles out on the periphery of the city's core in the late 1950s and the early 1960s

(Montejano 2010; Valdez n.d.).[18] Perhaps the hyper-locality of earlier groups from the downtown area contributes to this amnesia. It is also possible that the original groups from the Bounds area simply existed too long ago to be part of today's common corpus of barrio street-gang legends. Indeed, most of the participants in this era of the subculture are deceased, and many of the neighborhoods in the Bounds were wiped out or altered by urban reconstruction.

This raises several key issues regarding the structure and continuity of barrio networks. For instance, given that barrio gangs are thought to place high importance on neighborhood turf and tradition (Moore, Vigil, and Garcia 1983; Spergel 1990), to what extent was this true of San Antonio? Did the displacement of residents from the Bounds, the development of government-subsidized housing for low-income residents in the 1940s, or other social changes in the urban environment cause street gangs to undergo much change in network or organizational structure from one decade to the next? As in any large American city, the emergence and spread of these gangs from the core to other parts of the city follows the classical pattern depicted in social disorganization theory (Bursik and Grasmick 1993). An issue not addressed in the gang literature, however, is whether those original roots have any bearing on barrio processes in the newer locations gangs expanded to in subsequent generations.[19] Several of the mechanisms that potentially sustain such linkages are explored in a final section on intergenerational structure.

Intergenerational Barrio Dynamics

The classic works on barrio gangs depict them as intergenerational social groups, with older and younger siblings and fathers and sons often belonging to the same street gang in consecutive generations (Fleisher 1995; Moore 1978; Vigil 1988). In large cities, there is typically an age-graded hierarchy of *klikas* at the street level, beginning with pre-teen and early teen "peewee" sets, on to calotes in their late teens and early twenties (Vigil 1990). For most of the modern era, adult prison gangs have been at the top of the hierarchy, which has been the case in California (Davidson 1974) for much longer than in Texas (Fong 1990; Valdez 2005).

This study found at least three parent-child pairs that belonged to the same street gang in the Bounds in the 1950s. These were Los Wimpys from El Wesley barrio, Los Chachos from Los Cocos, and Los Quiros from the Boys Club. The sons in these pairs continued on in the street lifestyle in other barrios once the Bounds was disrupted and their families relocated. They fraternized with the groups in their new locality (most of whom they already knew), but they still represented their old gang's legacy. There were numerous other examples of father-son pairs and older-younger sibling pairs who kept up barrio traditions outside the Bounds as well (see chapter 4).

Of the various ethnic-based street gangs to emerge in America's slums over time, the barrio gang in particular is most noted for its turf-oriented character (Moore, Vigil, and Garcia 1983; Spergel et al., 2005). Compared to black or other ethnic street gangs, barrio gangs have always been more clearly defined by the neighborhoods where they originated than for their criminal "specialties" (Horowitz 1983; Moore et al. 1983; Vigil 1990). These intergenerational and hierarchical features created group longevity, making this ethnic gang population especially conducive to historical exploration.

A major caveat is that this archetype is based on southern California, where East LA barrio groups like Hoyo MaraVilla, White Fence, and Florencia 13 have been around since the 1940s and are still intact today. Similarly, gangs from the Logan Heights area in San Diego have been around for over fifty years. This phenomenon has not been well documented in Texas. Howard Campbell (2009) documented some of El Paso's multigenerational gangs in the Segundo Barrio, such as Los Fatherless, el Barrio Del Diablo, and Chihuahuita, some of which date back to the 1940s and were still intact as of the late 1990s. However, with regard to geography, culture, and family or other network ties, El Paso is closer to New Mexico, Arizona, and California than it is to the rest of Texas, and therefore Campbell's findings were not automatically generalizable to the rest of the state.

Montejano (2010) showed that like their LA and West Texas counterparts, San Antonio barrio gangs are also structured by place, space, and turf. His work captured multigenerational traditions, where some of the groups he chronicled from the late 1950s[20] lasted into the 1970s, 1980s, or 1990s.[21] Yet, as my current work shows, there were significant changes in barrio turf and tradition from the 1950s to the 1960s, when many of the original Chicano barrio groups died out, and new ones were born. This was due in part to urban redesign efforts in the Bounds and to new government housing projects in the inner West Side, such as the Cassiano and Mirasol homes, both built in 1953. Barrio discontinuity was evident when in the course of this study, 1950s research subjects scrutinized Montejano's (2010) work and were not familiar with several of the inner-city gang names he listed from the 1960s.[22] Also, most of the pre-1960s gangs of the Bounds were not documented in his work, nor was a large group from the far South Side called Varrio Palo Alto, or the North Side groups appearing in Figure 2 (e.g. Varrio Kenwood, Rattlesnake Hill).

The extent to which intergenerational barrio dynamics in San Antonio conform to the archetype in the literature is therefore underexplored. While a simplistic test, the most reliable indicator is the retention of barrio gang name and turf area over time. Using these criteria, all groups from the Bounds were multigenerational, some going back at least to the 1930s and lasting into the late 1950s and early 1960s, such as Riverside, Los Cocos, La Paloma, El Boys Club, and El West Side Bounds (a.k.a. Los Bounds). The group associated with the Wesley Community Center was also multigenerational, but in the 1970s the center was moved from the Bounds to the deep South Side, disrupting that forty- to fifty-year-old tradition. Groups from Government (Rattlesnake) Hill on the northern end of downtown also were documented as early as the 1920s and were still present in the 1950s and 1960s. By all appearances, none of these gangs existed past the early 1970s.

There is thus evidence of long-term barrio group name and turf retention in San Antonio, but it is limited to a few groups, and on average, the longevity period spans about thirty to forty years. A select few San Antonio barrio gangs have retained the same name and neighborhood turf boundaries for a longer period, however. In several cases, the groups date back to the 1940s and 1950s and are still intact today. The inner West Side gang Varrio La Blanca, which emerged in 1951 with the construction of the government-subsidized, low-income housing project, the San Juan homes, remained an intact group with prison gang ties until midway through the first decade of the 2000s.[23] Lalo Valdez (2005) documented an intense gang war occurring in the 1990s between this group and their rivals, the LA Boyz, from the nearby Mirasol and Cassiano housing projects. Meanwhile, Varrio Palo Alto and Varrio Grey Eagle are two long-time, on- and-off rivals from the far South Side. Each has been around since the 1940s or 1950s, and to the knowledge of this author (see chapter 7), are still intact today, evidencing at least some sixty-five years of longevity. Varrio Kenwood (established sometime during the 1940s) and the Lynwood Gang (established during the 1950s) are two longtime rival barrio groups to the north of downtown who are also still likely to be intact.

These findings result from using the most superficial criterion for barrio longevity, gang name and turf area retention. However, there are cases that defy such simplistic criteria, but that are still worth analyzing within the general framework used here. For example, how should we consider modern groups who claim the turf of a past generation, but who have undergone one or more changes in barrio (gang) name and structure? Consistent with social disorganization theory (Bursik and Grasmick 1993; Kornhauser 1978), unless they are gentrified, local conditions that sustain gangs in certain parts of town tend to be consistent over time. There are therefore modern groups with a significant number of members who are descendants or younger relatives of long-time residents whose gangs have controlled that barrio's turf for decades, but the younger generation has changed the name and structure of the gang.

One such case involves one of the best-known 1950s-1970s San Antonio barrio groups called "Ghost Town" in the deep West Side. By the 1980s their turf was claimed by a group called Bad Company, a.k.a. the BCs. From all appearances, many of the members were descendants of the Ghost Town members from a prior era, but their structure and style of governance was far different from that of their predecessors, consistent with "modernized" gang norms (see chapter 7). The appropriate way to categorize or interpret such outcomes using the intergenerational archetype is not quite clear. In an interesting twist, after the BCs disintegrated in the early 2000s and left a vacuum, according to San Antonio area juvenile gang officers and various youth living in the area, the next youth cohort readopted the Ghost Town name (Varrio Ghost Town, VGT) in about 2010. At this point, it was not known to what extent there were original kinship or other network ties to the 1950s group—which raises a related point about requirements for membership in future generations of barrio gangs.

Moore et. al. (1983) examined the question of whether residency within the barrio's turf was a requirement for barrio membership in East LA. They found that a significant number of youth who were full-fledged members of certain groups did not live on the barrio's turf. The reasons for this were varied, such as family relocation, lengthy incarcerations, being from an adjacent area, having a preference for the gang's reputation, or having been recruited in school, jail, or prison, and joining the gang upon release. These organic processes were also found in San Antonio. In fact, in the 1950s, before the era of strict gang member initiations, there were many barrio dwellers with multiple gang affiliations. As discussed in chapter 1, accurately listing gang member names became challenging when certain individuals were associated with different gangs through these varied circumstances. These issues are discussed further within the context of barrio network size, family ties, incarceration, drug use, and addiction in the following chapter.

Three
The Paradoxes of Barrio Gang Networks

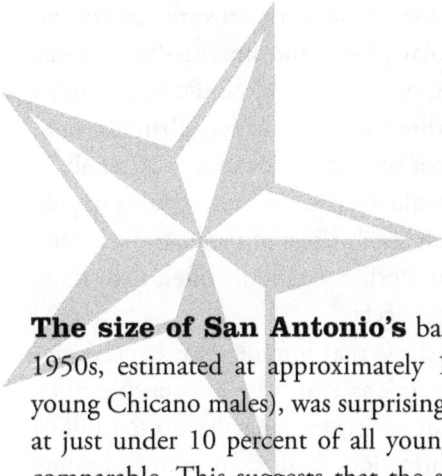

The size of San Antonio's barrio youth gang population in the 1950s, estimated at approximately 1,300 persons (8.5 percent of all young Chicano males), was surprisingly finite. Then, the 2007 estimate, at just under 10 percent of all young Chicano males, was remarkably comparable. This suggests that the size of the youth gang population may be constant in this specific community.[24] That the relative size of the barrio gang population is so comparable in both eras has important sociological implications that are revisited throughout this work.[25] To begin this chapter, however, I ponder whether the *absolute* size of the group estimates matters more than *relative* size for issues related to the barrio's network structure.

There may have been a discernible network among San Antonio's barrio gangs of the 1950s that can no longer be analyzed meaningfully because of the city's sheer growth in area and population over the last half century, This echoes, in part, Lefty's Durkheimian observation in chapter 2 about the loss of community over the years. Hypothetically, if we had complete information on all connections that existed between individuals in the 1950s and year 2007 data presented in chapter 1, and diagrammed the network structure of the barrio in each era, what should we expect to find? One hypothesis is that the network density in the 1950s would be higher (i.e., more connectivity among individuals) than in 2007. However, as theorized by social network scholars, odds are that the quantified measure of a social system's density will increase with its size due to its higher capacity for connections (Faust 2006). The key question then becomes: can today's Chicano gang network in San

Antonio be regarded as the same type of system as the 1950s network, or perhaps as a derivative of it?

To consider the possibility that modern Chicano gang networks have similar qualities to those of the 1950s, I briefly address the effect of recent advances in communication technology on modern network density. For example, the common use of cellular phone and internet-based social media in modern gang networking may help to close the connectivity gap in a growing society. On the other hand, it may exacerbate the anonymity and "noise" that comes with a large, complex society. After all, in the lower classes where gangs predominate, the most affordable pre-paid versions of cell phones are commonly used. Users of these products tend to experience the loss of contacts and other data more often than those with more stable subscriptions and gadgets.

Another development in this vein is that internet-based social networking creates long-distance connections that were implausible in an earlier time. For the past decade or so, street gangs have used online social networking sites to post information about their groups, leading to the spread of gang subculture in both superficial and consequential ways. Around the middle of the first decade of the 2000s, street gangs began using the online platform Myspace.com to post information about their gang, which served to glorify this lifestyle to young Internet users who stumbled upon or purposely sought out those sites. This medium has therefore been used to recruit youth to gangs, to intimidate or create conflict with rival groups (local or distant), and to network with those in distant places who are natural allies under the same gang "nation," (e.g., crip, blood, folk). This practice has even been known to facilitate communication between street gangs and Mexican drug cartels (Womer and Bunker, 2010).

These issues in the use of networking technology by gangs are revisited throughout the book, as subsequent chapters continue to compare the structural characteristics of Chicano gangs in past and modern eras. Without the comprehensive data needed to test any hunches about the effect of barrio network size on its density in the modern era, I build a foundation for our theoretical expectations using the data available. The issue is addressed with qualitative data provided by 1950s study participants on their own lives, on those of their families and peers, and on the general characteristics of the network for that era. Here and in the remaining chapters, I begin to describe a patchwork of ex-cons, addicts, pimps, prostitutes, drug bosses, their employees and enforcers, and other street criminals, and how they all related to or interconnected with each other.[26]

The data demonstrate that individuals with varied life circumstances had common ties to an intense barrio gang scene as teens, and experienced immensely varied trajectories as adults. This questions the notion that the underclass model so often used in the recent literature on young, impoverished slum dwellers fits the case of poor, urban, Chicano delinquents in the 1950s. It also speaks to the wide variation in those gang members' levels of human and social capital. In layman's terms, this group may not all be cut from the same cloth, which challenges theoretical notions about the role of a low self-control trait in producing serious or chronic offenders, and the connection of these concepts to that of the criminal class.

The Scale and Characteristics of Barrio Networks

Having established that the scale of the barrio street-gang phenomenon was much smaller in the 1950s than it is today, I must now clarify a few points. My use of the term *network* is not meant to suggest the extent to which gang members were unified across the city, or that I intend to focus solely on their alliances. It refers to the extent to which they simply all knew and interacted with each other, if not personally, then through intermediaries or common associates. This would also include the violent or otherwise negative interactions they had with each other, interactions that imply they knew each other or knew *of* each other, if not at the time of conflict, then eventually. It also includes knowing by reputation, via the *alambre* (wire) referred to in chapter 1. When conceptualized in this way, the view that it was a qualitatively different experience in the 1950s than it is today may be less defensible, as these interactions remain salient ways to develop reputations among the gang population. The alambre of today, however, not only includes word-of-mouth but cell phone texting and online social networking.

In the course of the fieldwork conducted for the 1950s portion of this book, nearly all interviewees personally knew all 475 others named in the research or had at least heard of them. Moreover, the same names continued to surface in discussions about who were the most reputable street persons in various parts of town. While these are simple earmarks, they tend to support the idea that in this context, a smaller scale increases the density of the network. Although that type of familiarity among members of the Chicano gang "universe" in San Antonio seems unlikely today, this idea is only a hypothesis, as there is no apparent feasible study design to properly investigate it. Nonetheless, the benefit of exploring these issues wherever one can is that it informs us of the systems shaping the social spheres or parameters of the network.

These parameters include residential/spatial proximity, biological and fictive kinship, institutional settings, drug addiction as a shared human condition or adaptation, the work setting, romantic relationships, leisure, and "business." The latter two items are intertwined, as they may equate to leisure time spent in legitimate barrio businesses such as "sock hops" (*los bailes*), or drive-in theaters, which attracted youth from all barrios. This is where many gang fights and other reputation-forming events occurred. In early adulthood, "leisure" time is merged with "business" in that it might include time spent at one of numerous and infamous barrio club (bar) hangouts for gangsters and wise guys. These issues are treated more thoroughly in chapters 4 and 5, with discussions about who were important persons in the barrio network, where they hung out, and why they were so reputable. In the social networks literature, such central nodes, or key players, have many connections and/or occupy an important position in the network (Borgotti 2006). I describe how their barrio street gang days relate to their illegitimate and often lucrative business dealings as adults.

Kinship

One compelling research finding in support of a criminal-class network hypothesis is that of the several hundred barrio gang members named for the 1950s era, about 40 percent are composed of pairs or groups of siblings. As the number of names collected, approximately 475, meets a commonly accepted sample size threshold for obtaining a respectable confidence level in the generalizability of the findings for a population of approximately 1,300 barrio gang youth (Bartlett, Kotrlik, & Higgins 2001), we can assume this percentage is close to the actual proportion of siblings in that universe. Also, there is no reason to expect that a different proportion of siblings would be found among barrio gang networks today, which is another parallel between network structure in both eras. There are also a large number of other kinship connections among the gang members, such as cousins, in-law relationships, and several father-son pairs in successive generations of the gang. Ironically, whereas much of the past research offers that the American street gang serves as a sur-rogate family for youth from disjointed or dysfunctional families (e.g. Decker & Van Winkle 1996), blood kinship among a large subset of its members is prominent in the network structure found here.

The Apple Often Does Fall Far from the Tree

One obvious mechanism in barrio network cohesiveness across the gen-erations is the continuity of criminal involvement by the children of the 1950s barrio members. To the extent that there is continuation of gang activity or other criminal identity by their offspring, this supports the notion of a criminal class. There is a notable track record of children following in the footsteps of their criminal parents in the literature on this topic (Besemer 2012; Farrington 2011; McCord 1991; Osborne and West 1979). The correlation between parental and child criminality is far from perfect, but as deviance predictors at the individual level go, it is quite strong. The measurements used, however, are typically very crude, as they mainly include arrests, convictions, and incarcerations. Most stud-ies simply match these statuses (yes/no) to those of the parents, with little attention to the level or type of criminal involvement of each. One caveat is that many of the total arrests and imprisonments in parent-child sam-ples occur among a small proportion of families, similar to the distribu-tion found among individual chronic offenders.

The predictors and mechanisms by which criminogenic transmission occurs between parents and children are well understood, to include ge-netics, low parental school performance, and for youth who spend time with their criminally-involved parents, exposure to domestic violence, overtly harsh discipline, parental emotional instability, and learning or modeling behavior (Farrington 2011). However, the broader social as-pects of the criminal behavior of parents vis-à-vis that of their children are not well captured by this literature. While implied by differential association theory, there is not much concrete insight in the literature on parent-child co-offending or replication of offense type. Rather, the transmission process is described as subtle and non-specific, as captured by the concept of criminal propensity. In fact, criminal fathers are more likely to verbally discourage their children from engaging in criminal conduct than to encourage them to follow their example (Farrington 2011).

The current work approaches such questions in terms of continuity of networks, delinquent groups, and lifestyle. I examine the implications of these elements for archetypal Chicano gang processes such as multigenerational barrio turf, hierarchy, and organizational continuity. This also implies the possibility of inverse outcomes, such as organizational discontinuity, hybridization, reorganization, intergenerational tension, and conflict. In a word, this study is concerned with barrio underworld politics, beginning with the family unit. Therefore, questions of heritability and micro-behavioral transference mechanisms that occur within the home are not of central concern here, and are not well addressed by the study's framework. Where incarceration was a common experience for much of the study's sample, many did not spend ample time actively raising their children, which questions the role of routine transference.

Still, there are two distinct ways in which the current research findings conceptually overlap with the mainstream work on parent-child criminality. First, in practical terms, the correlation between parental and child criminality is as weak as it is strong in the literature, where the strongest correspondence rates are about 60 percent for arrest and convictions (Farrington, 2011), and 50 percent for imprisonments (McCord 1991).[27] On the low end, the "delinquency" agreement rate is in the 15 to 20 percent range (Eddy and Reid 2001). That is, rates of parent-child criminality depend on where and how continuity is measured, but generally, it is more likely that children of criminogenic parents will *not* follow in their parents' path. Thus I draw as much attention to those outcomes, as well as "mixed" cases, as I do to those that exemplify intergenerational continuity. Secondly, where the study data contain examples of the role of arrest and incarceration in the state or federal prison system in the lives of parents and their children, it does make use of the typical outcomes found in the literature on this topic. However, the findings from this study evidence a much lower rate of parent-child agreement than what is found in the literature. Before advancing to family-based findings, it is important to point out some of the data-gathering dynamics involved.

Family Criminality as a Taboo Issue

Despite the study's purpose to provide a "big picture" perspective of San Antonio barrio networking processes, qualitative investigation of family issues is a difficult endeavor. To begin, there are near-universal norms regarding the family as a sacred institution, and the provision of unconditional support for one's children, which precludes placing them in a bad light to outsiders. These principles are especially salient among the 1950s generation, true also of most Latinos, who in the sociological research on work, migration, and overall lifestyle are characterized as being very family-oriented (Tienda and Mitchell 2006).

Although some of the intergenerational dynamics one would expect to find do emerge in the study's hermeneutics, it is difficult data to record and to gracefully write up. Elders often become defensive when one begins asking about the criminal histories and other lifestyle elements of their grown children or grandchildren. And while it may be an ethnic cultural norm more generally, it is often well-founded in the current context. In some cases, a male child was murdered due to their deep level of gang involvement or other criminal activity.[28] Many of the daughters, too, became deeply entrenched in drug use and other criminal associations. The grandchildren of the 1950s generation now range in age from school-aged children to adults in their early thirties; thus, shielding their crime-involved younger family members from a curious academic researcher is part of this dynamic.

Even outside of the criminological context, it is difficult to ask parents about the fate of their grown children, their lot in life, successes, failures, and lessons learned. Once enough trust and familiarity has been built with the subject to know about their kids, or even meet them, it remains somewhat taboo to qualitatively investigate and write about them. I circumvent this challenge by presenting a brief profile with only enough family information to draw inferences about whether crime "runs in families." Table 1 contains basic information about the criminogenic status of twenty-five research subjects, their siblings, and their children.

Table 1: Brief Profile of Subjects, Their Siblings, and Their Children's Life Outcomes

1950s Barrio Gang Member	Profile & Criminogenic Status	Siblings	Children
01	Parents from Mexico; non-drug user; no prison time; working class; bar owner; well known & respected in the barrio.	One brother a barrio gang member, but church oriented, pro-social in later life. Second brother a laborer, no criminal involvement. Sisters were "squares."	Three sons, no prison time, one military, all working class families.
02	Working class father; lifelong heroin user; 29 total years in prison; building tender[29]; no real work history outside of prison.	One brother murdered at age 18, other brother Air Force career, non-criminal, non-addict. Sister non-criminal, non-addict.	Four children, no high school graduates. One son currently in prison for drug trafficking; second son was an addict; one daughter was an addict; second daughter married, family, middle class Chicano lifestyle.
03	Early heroin user; high school grad, military, 8–9 years prison, then college graduate (cum laude), semi-professional career.	Sister also known in the barrio; younger brother non-criminal/non-gang member, Vietnam vet, retired sheriff's deputy.	One biological son, raised 3 adopted young children, each non-criminal outcomes.
04	Juvenile prison, military tour, adult prison, working-class laborer.	Brother was also well-known barrio gang member who went to juvenile and adult prison, became a minister.	Three sons: two addicts—one went to prison, became high-ranking gang members, one did not; one went into law enforcement, other children working class.

05	Early heroin user; adult prison, working-class laborer.	One brother did time, sisters were addicts, one brother clean.	One daughter a bar owner; second daughter is a nurse; one son a sheriff's deputy; second son a grocery store supervisor.
06	No prison, non-drug user, working-class laborer.	Sibling was a barrio gang member, construction worker, two trips to adult prison; died from a stabbing in prison; two other brothers "squares," WWII vets.	Son did some federal prison time, is an associate of a prison gang. Daughter high school grad; working class.
07	Orphaned; juvenile prison; adult prison; working class, subject passed away 2013.	One brother killed in a gang fight.	Two sons, no info on them.
08	Non drug-user, no juvenile prison; military career, no adult prison, bar owner, shop owner	Brother went to prison for murder at age 19; another sibling was murdered; third brother an influential member of adult barrio underworld.	Eight kids total, all high school graduates, some college graduates, all working/middle class families.
09	Non-drug user; Military service, no prison; well-known barrio member. Working-class laborer.	No siblings	Two sons, one daughter, non-criminal, "good jobs."
10	Working class, no prison; pleaded to a trafficking case late in life.	Brother currently in prison.	Seven kids with multiple women, "none turned criminal."

continued

1950s Barrio Gang Member	Profile & Criminogenic Status	Siblings	Children
11	Juvenile prison; working class, no adult prison.	Youngest of 11 children, varied life outcomes for siblings.	Three sons: one is a sheriff's deputy; other two sons working class. Two daughters, one had prison gang ties, went to prison for drug trafficking; one is in law enforcement.
12	Military career; drug trafficker, no prison.	Four brothers; one sister; all "squares."	Two kids, college graduates.
13	Orphan; lifelong heroin user; military service; several prison terms totaling 20 years; killed in pedestrian accident 2017.	Several siblings, no contact with them. Subject claimed most were non-criminal.	Nine children from five women; one prison gang member.
14	Juvenile prison; trucker, other working class jobs, no adult prison.	Brother went to juvenile prison, adult prison, gang member; another brother was also a gang member.	Two criminal sons, two non-criminal/mixed outcomes. One daughter living in Midwest, non-criminal to mixed.
15	Lifelong heroin user; 13 total years in prison.	Brother was a barrio gang member, assaulted, died.	One addict daughter, one hyper-religious daughter.
16	Laborer, currently in prison on a life sentence.	One sister, non-criminal.	Three children from three different women, one born in Chicago; estranged, not much known about their outcomes but generally non-criminal.

17	Vietnam vet, heroin user since then. Was on the area's most wanted list in 1974 for drug trafficking, prison sentence, passed away 2013.	One brother, middle class, non-user, no prison.	No children.
18	Four trips to adult prison 25-30 total years; life term, ten straight years.	Three siblings, all working class & semiprofessional.	Three kids, no college, one works for the city, "good job."
19	Lifelong heroin user, 17 years in prison; GED in prison, screen printer/graphic design; father was law enforcement.	Three brothers, two non-convicts, one brother "did some time," one was a marine, became a postman.	Two kids, same wife, divorced; boy became a parole officer, daughter did 5 years in prison.
20	Crime-involved family; working class laborer; bar owner; young heroin dealer/user; federal prison.	Brother murdered in his late 20s in Chicago.	One son, police officer; one daughter non-criminal; second son lives in Chicago.
21	Juvenile prison for murder age 15; 30 total years in adult prison over five trips. Became a machine-shop instructor in a community college.	No brothers, one sister, "square."	One son, professional class; two daughters, non-criminal.

continued

1950s Barrio Gang Member	Profile & Criminogenic Status	Siblings	Children
22	Father was a photographer; subject spent 18 total years in adult prison; lifelong drug use; no work history; prisoner rights activist.	Three sisters "squares"; one brother lifelong prison sentence for murder; one brother died of overdose.	One biological son, no criminal involvement, certified chef.
23	Father in the military; mom worked in hospital; juvenile prison, spent half his adult life in prison.	Two sisters, "squares," working class husbands; one niece did 10 years in prison for drug sales; her husband also belonged to the street subculture.	One son just released from prison; three other sons murdered for involvement in prison gang activity.
24	Juvenile prison, spent half of his adult life in prison, heroin user.	Four brothers, all non-criminal outcomes.	One daughter, non-criminal outcome.
25	No juvenile prison; parents from rural county; broken home, raised by grandmother, marines, spent half of his adult life in prison.	Four brothers, mixed outcomes, all went into the military and most also went to prison. All brothers were boxers, some with professional aspirations.	One son, marine corps, mostly non-criminal profile, employed in quasi-legal underground gambling industry.

Family-Based Findings

While the findings on gang involvement by siblings and extended kin discussed earlier in the chapter illustrate one aspect of familial connections within barrio gang networks, other family-related facets become apparent when examining a more detailed set of criminogenic information on subjects and their family members in Table 1 above. To summarize these findings, eight of the twenty-five subjects (32 percent) in this subset went to state school (prison) as juveniles, and seventeen of the twenty-five (68 percent) went to prison as adults. Of fifty-eight siblings, only eighteen (31 percent) either went to prison, were addicts, or led a criminal lifestyle.

The remaining siblings showed a varied set of life paths and outcomes, mainly staying within the working class, and having done a good share of public service. At least seven (12 percent) served in the military, and several became law enforcement officers.

Of some eighty-one children fathered by this subsample of 1950s-era barrio gang members, only thirteen (16 percent) went to prison, reinforcing the conclusion that intergenerational continuity of criminal behavior within the family is far from guaranteed, at least by this measure. Indeed, half as many that went to prison went into law enforcement occupations. Eight or nine of their children (about 10 percent) were in prison gangs, five were murdered or died of a drug overdose, five or six went on to college, another five or six were law enforcement officers, and most went into the working class.

This brief profile illustrates the varied criminogenic statuses of the men in the study, and the wide range of life outcomes among them, their siblings, and their children. These findings run contrary to the notion of a monolithic underclass or criminal class that so many theorists and law enforcement practitioners assume exists in the populations they study or work with. It also speaks to the nuanced way in which human and social capital interacts with the criminal element, and how difficult criminal involvement is to measure or predict. The proportions of siblings and children leading criminal lifestyles were not very large, which is not quite consistent with findings showing significant sibling similarity (e.g. Lauritson 1993) or intergenerational transmission on this dimension. As described in the next section, a big part of this discussion has to do with the notion of social class.

On Crime and Social Class

Good measurements of social class are elusive in the social sciences. The standard barometers are income and wealth, education level, occupational prestige or industry, and homeowner or renter status. These may be useful when applied to broad population segments, but they do not capture the class variation within neighborhoods that are very homogenous on most of these indicators. Nor do these measures account for cultural and behavioral features that are part of gauging social class (e.g. family size, criminal history, welfare dependency, children from multiple fathers, drug use, child protection involvement). In this regard, Elijah Anderson's (1993) notion of the continuum of *street* and *decent* family styles within the ghetto is perhaps more useful as an analytical concept for measuring social class in the barrio.

Reflecting Ruth Kornhauser's (1978) claim that whole neighborhoods or subcultures did not value crime and violence, over time barrio families are inclined to become decent or non-criminal if they can, or at least to camouflage themselves as such. A large or extended family's position on the street-to-decent continuum depends on a host of things like where they live, how they earn their living, their age composition, family gang ties, etc. There is lots of variation among barrio families on the street-to-decent continuum, and it is often dynamic.

On one end of the continuum are those families with no real roots in the barrio gang scene, and no family members who have ventured very far off in that direction (i.e., purely *decent*). In other cases, formerly street-oriented families have shaken the association after several generations of assimilation into the mainstream. And still in other cases, there was a single black sheep of the family who gravitated to the street subculture, but the family's association to the street was not strong.

Some families are truly criminogenic, with successive generations in prison and drug and gang ties in and out of prison (i.e. purely *street*). Depending on other circumstances like family income, welfare dependency, etc., these are often the families we equate with lower-class or underclass status. However, as the age composition and other circumstances of the extended family change, these ties may weaken; then with a new generation coming of age, ties to the street and prison can become strengthened after a hiatus. Therefore, the nexus between social class and criminal involvement is changeable, and is often dynamic. Table 1 reflected the numerous combinations of features along the street-to-decent continuum in the barrio.

Incarceration

A salient aspect of the gang network structure to emerge in the study relates to the bonds that form or clashes that occurred in the shared incarceration experience. There are several contexts in which this occurred for San Antonio barrio youth found to be delinquent by the juvenile courts. The first is temporary incarceration (i.e. pre-adjudication lockup) in a county facility. In San Antonio, the Bexar County Training School for Boys in a far south portion of the city (a.k.a. "Southton") served this purpose since at least the 1930s (*San Antonio Express-News* 1939) and likely for several decades prior. As is the case today (albeit in a newer, centralized facility), delinquent boys from around the county were locked up together when arrested by the police to await a hearing for release or the setting of a court date. There, boys from various neighborhoods met, either forming alliances or rivalries, sometimes based on prior interactions on the street.

A second context for association by boys deemed by the court to be chronic or serious offenders was the state-level school, i.e. "reform" school, known then as the Texas Youth Council, and today as the Texas Juvenile Justice Department. The photo below, taken at Gatesville State School for Boys (Texas) in 1954, is a group of boys from San Antonio. Several of them were subjects in the current study and in some cases were from rival gangs. Yet in the state school setting, where there are boys of other races and from other parts of the state, subjects said that they banded together based on their ethnicity and hometown. This perhaps represents one of the earliest forms of the *Tango* gang subculture that is now dominant in Texas jails and prisons (chapter 6 contains a detailed description of the modern forms of these city-ethnic based alliances). Once released, boys who knew each other in the incarceration setting were more prone to form either cross-barrio alliances or to offer mutual respect for having shared the incarceration experience and having banded together against non-San Antonio groups or non-Chicanos.[30]

Later, many young men who were incarcerated together as youth, along with many others they didn't know, would meet up in county jail and in state or federal prison. There, again, interactions among inmates or statuses held while incarcerated created rivalries, alliances, and reputations, which followed them out into the streets when released. For example, in

Los vatos en la corre juvenil. Youth at the Gatesville School for Boys. *Courtesy of the personal photo collection of Mr. Brijido Minjares Jr. of San Antonio.*

the 1960s and 1970s, Texas state prisons used thirty to thirty-five-man work crews in the fields, which required lots of cooperation among the inmates. Some friendships that were formed there often lasted a lifetime ("Hippo," Taco Village).

Up until the early 1980s, Texas prisons used the building tender system to keep control of inmates. This was a trustee system that relied on influential, respected inmates to police other inmates (Fong 1990). Although it was highly effective, it was challenged and ruled unconstitutional in federal district court in 1980. While they were chosen for their ability to manage the inmate population with fairness, being a building tender also came with negative repercussions, as evident in the inmate nickname used to describe the role, "*marrano*" (pig). Many who assumed this role became the target of violence both in and out of prison.

Tensions and conflicts among the 1950s barrio generation that occurred into the 1960s and 1970s are addressed in subsequent chapters.

Texas-based inmates at Leavenworth, Kansas, Federal Penitentiary, 1961. *Courtesy of Gilbert "Hippo" Carranza* (front row, far left) *of San Antonio.*

Indeed, people who did time together would later target each other in "the free" due to a falling out over a debt owed, a family member's actions, a disagreement, a misunderstanding, prison gang affiliations, old prison "beefs," and in some cases, over seemingly minor disputes stemming from machismo as a cultural norm. The remainder of this chapter addresses several other systems that condition the barrio network and continue to exemplify the surprisingly high levels of social capital that certain members had.

Drug Addiction as a Binding Force

An interviewee named "El Juan Chota" is proud to list the few members of his group and other gang associates *"que no se tiraban"* (who didn't shoot heroin), suggesting that it was common in the 1950s street scene. In his investigative journalistic work on the 1970s heroin trade in San Antonio, Wilson McKinney (1975) revealed that heroin began to hit the street most prominently there in the 1940s, naming *Los Bounds* as its epicenter. Still, that boys in their mid-teens were injecting heroin in the early 1950s suggests that it was a rather intense subculture for such an early stage in barrio street-gang history. One of my requests to subject collaborators was for them to create lists of well-known "hypos" (heroin shooters) and of "ex-*pintos*" (former inmates) in their midst. As might be expected, the degree of overlap among the two groups was great, and the implications for barrio networking processes are poignant.

> "*Tecatos* (heroin users) would meet in jail or prison and would form connections city-wide to be able to score when they got out. So they could go into various territories to score, but usually it was just "in and out," cause you *were* from another area, so you couldn't just hang out in any barrio for too long."
>
> ("El Black Sam," Los Luckeys)

As described earlier in this chapter, there was a rather large subset of youth named in the research who either belonged to more than one barrio, in terms of groups claiming the individual, or who associated with more than one. No doubt this is partly because of what Sam relayed above. Two other subjects, "Polo" of Barrio Columbus and "El Mysterio" (The Circle and El Alto) separately said that "*gracias a Dios* (thank God), I could go into various barrios to conduct business." From this expression it appears that relations between barrios could be tenuous. The ability to move into other barrios is counter to what most of the literature on Chicano gang norms suggests about the importance of territoriality in the barrio. But like prison networking, drug networking often transcended barrio turf boundaries, something also found by Campbell (2009) in El Paso. This is a prism-like aspect of our observations of the barrio: what comes to light depends on one's perspective. The role of the drug trade in barrio networking is addressed again in the next chapter describing several barrio kingpins from the 1930s onward.

Barrio Unity via Employment

Chapter 2 noted that boyhood street-corner cliques in the Bounds often hustled shoeshines, sold newspapers together, and the like. As the families of 1950s youth in poverty did not benefit from social welfare programs to the extent that modern poor families do, barrio youth of that era developed a work ethic within the legitimate labor force that is rare to see in today's gang youth. For older teens and young adults in the barrio, two well-known work-related settings that served as the context for barrio identification were La Tripa and La Piedrera. La Tripa was the meat-processing district situated in the inner West Side. It employed young men and women from the area, many of whom frequented the various hangouts and bars in the area such as El Tompay, Packers, and Blue Heaven. Youth from this barrio who worked in the factories carried around a leather holster called a *voucha* for a set of knives used in their trade, and would use them if needed in a bar fight with another barrio (Pilinga, Alazan/La Tripa). Similarly, the barrio La Piedrera emerged from a Mexican work-camp area called Cementville, built specifically for laborers in San Antonio's rock quarry north of downtown (Dunn 1997). The small neighborhood's main street was Pastores Drive, where boys whose families worked in the quarry congregated. Starting in the late 1950s, this group also identified itself as "RQ," and the group remained active well into the 1990s, perhaps even into the 2000s.

Military and Law Enforcement Connections

An impressive subset of persons named as having belonged to San Antonio's barrio gang subculture went on to enlist in military service. While only twenty-five names surfaced of 1950s barrio youth who definitively were in the military (about 5 percent of all names collected in the study), this was a piece of data that I began probing relatively late in the study. For this reason, it is sure to be a gross undercount, but relative to today's comparable figure,[31] is a significant portion nonetheless. A number of interviewees described their exit from the gang life as having been propelled by their enlistment in military service. In many cases, typically among influential gang youth, military enlistment was virtually forced upon them by local police. A recurrent story told by this portion of the sample is that lead officers in the juvenile bureau gave them the ultimatum to "go to the military or go to prison." These members described this as a strategy used by police to address the barrio's growing gang problem by extracting certain youths (namely the leaders) from the environment.

While not unheard of today, it is rare to find former gang members enlisted in the US military. Where it does happen, some analysts consider it strategic on the part of the gang to gain tactical and weapons knowledge by its members (National Gang Intelligence Center 2011).

Otherwise, military service is typically equated with honor, sacrifice, service to one's country, and other admirable traits. It therefore may surprise some to learn that the early adult experience of many 1950s barrio gang members included military service, but perhaps the recent connotation of the term "gang member" is to blame for that. It may be that the youth who gravitated toward barrio gang life in the 1950s are different from those of today, in terms of human capital, character, or potential. While ghetto and barrio youth gangs of today seem to conform more to the underclass model of street-oriented subjects (see Ricketts and Sawhill 1988), this characterization is not as applicable to much of the 1950s generation.[32]

Barrio Cops

Another interesting finding that exemplifies the paradox of gang membership and its counterintuitive network structure is that in at least ten known cases, a named gang member's father was a member of law enforcement. One former member of a reputable West Side gang who refused participation in the study is also a retired officer of the SAPD, well known for his narcotics detective work. What do such elements imply about the nexus of the barrio and the police? Clearly the barrio is a source of human capital for the police force, in that men who grew up there are quite often some of the best candidates to effectively police it. It is an interesting dichotomy that one family member can be a lifelong drug dealer/user, in and out of prison, while his biological parent or sibling is a police officer. It suggests that in the barrio there can be a fine line separating lawmen and lawbreakers in terms of life chances, friendship and kinship networks, and so on.

The issue of barrio kids becoming police officers also presents several ethical dilemmas for them. As police departments are complex organizations that develop their own working culture, some have higher levels of corruption than others. Recruitment of officers from the barrio is an interesting subtopic in this vein. When one compares officer recruitment practices at the San Antonio Police Department and the Bexar County Sheriff's Office to their counterparts in Dallas, Houston, and Austin, for example, a larger proportion of San Antonio officers are said to be "homegrown" (Arguello 2013; Ryan 2012). While being from the barrio can help one's law enforcement career, and can create resentment, respect, or fear of such an individual among the criminal class, it is a double-edged sword in that it also increases the chances of police corruption. Various old truisms like "one must think like a criminal" clearly embody part of good police work, but at the risk of overusing such clichés, this is also a "slippery slope."[33]

Another dynamic in the police-barrio nexus is that just as in the ghetto, levels of trust and confidence in the police are typically low in the barrio (Duran 2009; Armaline et al. 2014). Therefore, Chicano officers are perceived by most barrio street types as *vendidos* (sellouts) who practice oppression against their own people. Chicano officers must learn to manage or counter this sentiment with good will to be effective, or else live with that perception and risk acquiring a negative reputation. In the same way that criminals develop reputations in the barrio, so do police officers, for better or for worse.

Paradoxical Networks, Human and Social Capital

The fact that street-savvy Chicanos form bonds while in service to their country and community and that profiles of members of the same family are criminologically varied both speak to issues of human capital. Generally, this refers to a person's character, their potential, their intelligence, their life chances, and their life choices; in a word, it is one's *value*.[34] Gang members are often regarded by the general public and by law enforcement to be lacking in all of these areas. While this viewpoint may be more defensible when observing the modern era's street-gang population, who are notoriously unequipped for success in the legal labor market (Western 2006), this was generally less true of youth that gravitated toward barrio street gangs in the past.

In the pre-1960s era, the word *gang* was not used by San Antonio barrio youth to describe their street corner societies. While used by the press to describe these groups in the 1950s, among Chicanos throughout the southwest, the loose synonym for *gang* was the word "barrio" (Mirandé 1987; Montejano 2010; Moore 1978; Vigil 1990). This often took the form of *los vatos del barrio,* i.e., the "neighborhood fellas," which for poor Chicanos was the street-based peer group that, at times, engaged in fights or other forms of delinquency together, but mostly just passed the time in normative ways.

Historically, the barrio youth gang population is a small segment of the community, which is street-smart at best and criminally violent at worst. As shown in Table 1, it is far from being a monolithic class, strata, or type of person that became involved with a barrio gang in the 1950s era, and barrio group activities have a very broad range of delinquent severity. It is also clear that the barrio gang, with its century-old history in San Antonio and many other Southwestern cities, is an institution that has undergone much change over time. Remaining chapters continue to address the intensity of barrio gangs, old and new, the contexts for networking among its participants, and issues in the human and social capital thereof.

Summary

This chapter began by contemplating whether the size of the barrio gang universe matters for network density. While various hypotheses were considered, the most intuitive conclusion is that the smaller scale of the 1950s environment created a qualitatively denser network than would be plausible today. Significant population growth and a proportional increase in the number of Chicano street gangs in San Antonio over time, coupled with the shorter lifespan of most youth street gangs today, surely decreases the interconnectedness of the overall gang population. Conditioned by various institutional forces in the community, the limited nature of earlier networks created barrio longevity for several decades, and in some cases even longer.

Intergenerational continuity of barrio gang participation within the family proves to be more complex and nuanced than expected, however. Information on the family members of a subsample of 1950s barrio gang members showed no clear patterns involving their siblings, where only about one third of them were also delinquent. The children of the subsample were not remarkably criminogenic, either. There were low agreement rates on criminal transference on all measures. Some cases were clear outliers, with multiple murders experienced because of prison gang involvement, which again speaks to the wide variation within the family outcomes in a sample of barrio youth.

While intergenerational continuity is certainly evident in some cases, it is often a touchy subject for interviewees, making this substantive material difficult to gather and present. Aside from the natural defensiveness of the elder generation on family matters, the prison-gang context becomes part of the story of continuity into the violent 1980s, keeping the topic somewhat taboo and off-limits to academic researchers. And few want to relive or discuss openly the painful reminders of murder, drug addiction, lengthy prison terms, or the like. Younger members of the family also often glorify the gangster identity, which draws them into this lifestyle, and older family members shield their inmate or gang-member status from outsiders. Thus while cogent examples of the importance of family in networking and generational continuity exist, this aspect of the study provides the least compelling case for it, compared to the data on other parameters of network structure.[35]

Incarceration is clearly an important networking context for barrio streetgangs in adolescence and adulthood. For families deeply entrenched in crime lifestyles, this experience tends to be normative, perhaps as much because certain families are labeled criminal by law enforcement as for any other reason (Bernburg , Krohn, & Rivera, 2006; Farrington 2011). For these families, experiencing incarceration could be considered a rite of passage, as arrest is nearly inevitable, given the family's reputation and criminal history. The war on drugs and mass incarceration that followed ensnared many barrio youth who used drugs. The incarceration setting tends to bring individuals together who, because of barrio loyalties, would not otherwise fraternize outside of the state school or prison. The same often occurs among drug users, addicts, and dealers. Incarceration and drug elements thus serve to mitigate the turf tradition of strict adherence to *barrio*, thereby transcending this neighborhood-based norm.

While most of the frameworks that form the barrio network are typical street-crime parameters (poverty, family and neighborhood traditions, incarceration, and drug addiction), several atypical elements also condition it. Subjects' ties to the workplace, the military, and police service are some of the more surprising elements of the networks and experiences of 1950s barrio gang youth. These counterintuitive frameworks have hinted that predicting pre-1960s barrio gang membership is something of a "black box." Other than ethnicity, poverty, and to some extent, drug use, one would find it difficult to identify selection mechanisms for barrio gang membership in this era. This chapter alluded to the varying levels of human and social capital found among the 1950s barrio gang generation, demonstrating this with family outcomes and other examples relating to the individual subjects' own trajectories.[36]

This finding of normative human capital potential among 1950s barrio gang members is especially interesting in light of the intensity of their gang subculture. The next chapter shows that levels of delinquent intensity were much higher than expected for the 1950s era. This presents a challenge to the notion of a criminal class, because one might expect for members of this highly delinquent subculture to be more homogenous in their family backgrounds and life outcomes. Interestingly, nearly identical proportions (approximately 10 percent) of young Chicano males in the 1950s and 2007 cohorts were part of the gang subculture, and this figure is only slightly higher than chronic offender proportions in the literature (approximately 7 percent). Thus, while the criminal propensity of the 1950s barrio gang member seems to have been high, their social capital and potential for upward mobility was far from homogenous. In the end, there is still much to learn about chronic offenders and gang members, perhaps in the context of period effects, where modernity has a certain impact on lower class youth.

Four
Social Spheres and the 1950s Barrio Subculture

Several broad frameworks shaping the network structure of the 1950s barrio gang universe were described in previous chapters. This chapter addresses some of the important remaining contexts for defining and giving substance to the barrio gang scene. The chapter begins with a discussion of the intensity of the subculture. The housing projects where many barrio gangs formed in the late 1940s and early 1950s and in many cases continued for decades are then profiled. In most cases, the gangs identified themselves by the housing project itself in name, turf, and membership criteria.

Other key contexts for gang activity were popular youth hangouts such as shoeshine stands, neighborhood cafés, *bailes* (dance halls) or impromptu *chankleos* (dances), drive-in theaters, and other staging areas near downtown that attracted youth from all barrios. Here is where much social posturing, gang fighting, and other reputation-forming events occurred. This chapter also profiles many of the well-known and central figures in the barrio landscape and some of the impactful events that constitute part of the urban lore of the 1950s era.

The Intensity of 1950s Barrio Gangs

One myth that my 1950s-era subjects want me to dispel in my writings about them is that they were more innocuous and their gangs less organized than their modern counterparts. They claim that while they may not have had the formal structure and weapons of gangs in subsequent decades, their loyalties to the gang and street lifestyle were just as intense, and their street

codes were just as well defined. Most anyone who heard about or who publicized the current research project assumed that the barrio gangs from the
1950s era were far more benign than their modern manifestations.[37]

Whether barrio gangs were more violent or fierce in the 1950s versus
the 1960s is a regular debate among the many people who helped to
inform the contents of this book. Naturally, men who were teens in the
1950s era will argue for their decade, while those from the 1960s generation argue for theirs. In terms of empirical data on the matter, Ramiro
Martinez (2014) studied Chicano homicides in San Antonio over time
and concluded that 1950 was a more violent era for Chicano males ages
16-24 than it was for the next cohort in 1960. This demographic group
accounted for a large portion of murder victims in the city in both eras,
but 1950 levels were slightly higher. Although his work lends insight to
the question of which decade produced the most violent deaths among
young males, his data do not capture gang-related homicides per se; thus
we are left to infer that the 1950s barrio gang scene was more violent—a
very reasonable assumption.

The popular notion that 1950s gangs were less lethal than those of
the 1960s and beyond is driven, in part, by recognition of the rudimen-
tary nature of the "tools of the trade" used in the 1950s. These sentiments
were expressed by two separate authors whose work was mentioned in
chapter 1. In his unpublished work on San Antonio's Chicano gangs of
the 1950s and 1960s, Roy Valdez (an expert gang interventionist and
social worker) discussed the weaponry as less lethal in the 1950s. Most
gang boys in the 1950s were still using homemade zip guns, for example. While potentially dangerous in an up-close encounter, the weapon
was generally not accurate; it malfunctioned often; and it was not likely
to be deadly unless it was a very "lucky" shot. Several interviewees described how in the 1950s, the reputation of the West Side group La India quickly changed after the gang burglarized a pawnshop and acquired
"real guns" (Pilinga, Alazan and Black Sam, Los Luckeys). Montejano
(2010) also discussed the role of increased access to vehicles and weapons
in the 1960s, making drive-by shootings more common and decreasing
the likelihood of apprehension by police.

There was plenty of coverage of juvenile gangs by local newspapers in
the 1950s, and it was depicted as a serious social problem. For example,

Det. Leonard "Toto" Salas of SAPD Juvenile Bureau with knives, chains, brass knuckles, and zip guns confiscated from barrio gang youth, 1956.
Courtesy San Antonio Express *Newspaper photo archives at UTSA's Institute of Texan Cultures.*

recall in chapter 2 the newspaper's description of Riverside and Espiga as dangerous, secretive West Side gangs in 1950. The following year, the Bexar County District Attorney conducted a citywide "gang inquiry," entailing a comprehensive probe into San Antonio's youth gangs. This required convincing a grand jury that there were "organized groups of young hoodlums" operating throughout the city (*San Antonio Express-News* 1951 (b)). Numerous news stories scattered throughout the 1950s described the serious, violent crimes perpetrated by inner city gangs, which grew in intensity into the late 1950s. Below is a small sample of story headlines from the era with the barrio groups involved in parentheses.

"Youth Beaten by Young Gang" *SA Express-News* 1955. (Las Americas in the Bounds)

"Five Indicted in Shootings" *SA Express-News* 1957. (Ghost Town vs. El Alto)

"Boy Says Killing 'Nothing Personal'" *SA Light* 1957. (The Lake Gang vs. Ghost Town)

"Boy Gives up Gun" *SA Light* 1959 a. (Riverside vs. El Town)

"No. 5 Booked in Gang Killing" *SA Light*, 1960. (El Circle vs. La Dot)

The incident involving the shooting death of then-leader of Ghost Town Adolfo Galan, a.k.a. Black Diamond, by a member of the Lake Gang was among the most memorable incidents of late 1950s barrio warfare. The victim, age eighteen, was unarmed, sitting in a vehicle. He was shot in the face at pointblank range with a .38 pistol by Gavino Valdez, who was standing outside the vehicle. It made such an impact not only because of the shocking manner in which the shooting took place, but also because the victim was known for his charisma, his popularity, and because he was not considered to be a menacing figure ("Jesse," The Lake Gang). Such incidents contributed to what others have since referred to as a "moral panic" about Chicano gangs (Zatz 1987) lasting well into the 1960s in San Antonio, when some argue that barrio gangs proliferated and warfare intensified (Montejano 2010; Valdez n.d.). In terms of achieving legendary status within the urban barrio gang subculture, such dramatic incidents tended to immortalize the youth involved, and there are many such tales to draw upon. Several more of these appear throughout this chapter.

Considering the amount of attention the press and the community gave to barrio gangs as a social problem in this era, it is interesting to note law enforcement's take on the scope of the matter.[38] In 1950, Bexar County Juvenile Probation officers identified four West Side gangs (*San Antonio Light* 1950), one of which, Butterfly, only partially came to light in this study.[39] In 1960, police stated there were eight gangs in San Antonio, "most from

Adolfo "Black Diamond" Galan. *Courtesy Rudy, Mary, and David Galan.*

the south and west sides," and that most were loosely knit neighborhood groups exhibiting clannish behavior rather than well-organized groups (Roberts 1960). Roy Valdez's records from the Good Samaritan social services center in the West Side, however, documented at least thirty groups for the same period. There were hundreds of violent encounters between Ghost Town and twenty-seven other groups from throughout the West and South Sides between 1959 and 1967 (Montejano 2010). My research documents that most of these gangs, plus over thirty others, were active since before the 1950s. Altogether, this illustrates that with such secretive, dynamic groups, knowledge of a barrio group's existence, structure, and activities is very elusive, and will vary according to the perspective of the agency or investigator conducting the inquiry. This issue is illustrated again in chapter 7 with the profile of the 1980s and 1990s Chicano gangs in San Antonio.

Public Housing and Barrio Gangs

Previous chapters established that west downtown was the birthplace of the barrio gang subculture in San Antonio's old red-light district known as the Bounds. This pattern of ethnic street gang emergence from the city's core outward is typical for American cities (Bursik and Grasmick 1993; Thrasher 1936; Whyte 1943). The advent of urban public housing tenements has contributed greatly to the concentration of poverty and violence and the spread and intensification of the US street gang phenomenon (Holloway et al., 1998; McNulty and Holloway 2000). As in most other cities, San Antonio's first public housing projects were built near downtown in what is now the inner city. The San Antonio Housing Authority (SAHA) was established in 1937 with plans for the construction of five major housing projects. These were the "Alazan and Apache Courts for Mexican Americans, Lincoln Heights and Wheatley Courts for blacks, and Victoria Courts for whites" (Texas State Historical Association 2014).

Up until it began to be inhabited by more Chicanos around the late 1990s, the Wheatley Courts remained a black-dominated area for about fifty years.[40] Lincoln Heights, located in the deep West Side approaching the impoverished western outskirts called Las Colonias, has always had a mix of blacks and Chicanos, however, with the latter the predominant group today. Similarly, the Victoria Courts' ethnic transformation from a white to a Chicano housing project began almost immediately upon completion in 1942. The construction of seven other Chicano-dominated public housing projects soon followed these original four, and they are all scattered throughout the inner and deep West Side.[41] This had the lasting effect of concentrating Chicano poverty in the near West Side, which is still evident today. Along with the young age structure that is a constant feature of US Chicano populations (Gonzales-Baker 1996), it created a social environment extremely conducive to delinquent subculture formation. Below I profile the Chicano-dominant housing projects in San Antonio as they pertain to barrio gang phenomena.

Alazan-Apache Courts

Perhaps no single locale in San Antonio's history has been a more potent social context for barrio gang identity and activity than the Alazan-Apache Courts. Completed in 1941, the units housed just over five thousand tenants in 1,180 units by 1942. The project had its own library, health clinic, and social, recreational, and educational programs, and tenants were required to be US citizens (Zellman 1983). Historically, the central-west area of town between the Alazan and Apache Creeks was the Mexican slum with the worst living conditions; thus it was the obvious choice for the project site. The quality of life for residents and those in the immediate vicinity was much improved by this housing development, yet there was far more demand for the modern facilities than could be accommodated. This temporary bright spot was therefore nested within an ongoing environment of poverty, vice, and typical West Side social living conditions. It wasn't long before youth from the Alazan-Apache Courts began to readapt to the larger environment. After all, new housing alone doesn't replace the youths' barrio subculture orientation, their typical means of recreation, and their prior connections to other barrio youth who did not live in new housing. On the contrary, to the extent that the Alazan-Apache Courts represented a clearly defined neighborhood or community, the psychological effect of belonging to it increased a sense of nativism and territoriality that is already part of the barrio youth's mind-set. Moreover, where Chicano youth of this era still experienced discrimination at school, in the workforce, and in the larger society, street gang affiliation remained a form of ethnic identity and counterculture (Bogardus 1943; Moore 1978; Vigil 1988).

Research subjects from the Alazanes described a robust gang subculture that had developed as of the late 1940s and early 1950s. Also known simply as Los Courts, it was one of the largest barrio gangs of the era.[42] At that time, barrio gangs did not adhere to strict initiation rites or rules of membership. Any youth from the courts who practiced the unspoken street codes of toughness and group loyalty, who hung around the group, who was willing to prove himself in turf-related fights and abide by other street deviance norms of the day was considered a worthy member.[43] These informal codes of conduct were enough to give loose structure to the gang, but as described in chapter 3, there were also lots of cross-gang memberships or affiliations with other groups outside the courts, prompting the existence of a vast (citywide) barrio network where individual and group reputations were paramount.

Housing projects such as the Alazan-Apache are known for producing infamous barrio youth that would continue with a street lifestyle as adults or who would remain reputable figures in San Antonio's barrio underworld over time, whether as bar owner-operators, as prison gang members, as independent drug dealers, or for specializing in some other form of street crime. Even some who did not rise to a higher level of criminal sophistication or who may have died young became reputable for having made their mark on the subculture as teens. To this day, the Alazan remains a potent context for Chicano gang networks in San Antonio. This was especially true from the 1960s to the early 2000s. Modern housing authority regulations enforce a zero tolerance policy prohibiting gang activity, including on-site disturbances, and recent felons are barred from residing within the courts. Any of these are grounds for rental denial or eviction. As alluded to in chapter 3, however, one can expect that family connections of gang members to the Alazan or other projects will keep them tied to the courts in some subtle or covert manner.

Methods and Ground Rules for Individual Profiles

As large a barrio as the Alazan was, and as big as its reputation is, it is difficult to single out individuals to profile as being central players in that age-graded network, or in the larger scope of delinquent San Antonio barrio youth of the 1950s era. In the following sections, and throughout the remainder of this book, the approach used for mentioning or profiling individuals, incidents involving them, or other references to specific persons is based on the author's assessment, after three years of intensive fieldwork with surviving subjects, some of whom were among the most reputable.[44] That is, because the research is based upon the size and other characteristics of the barrio gang network, specific facts,

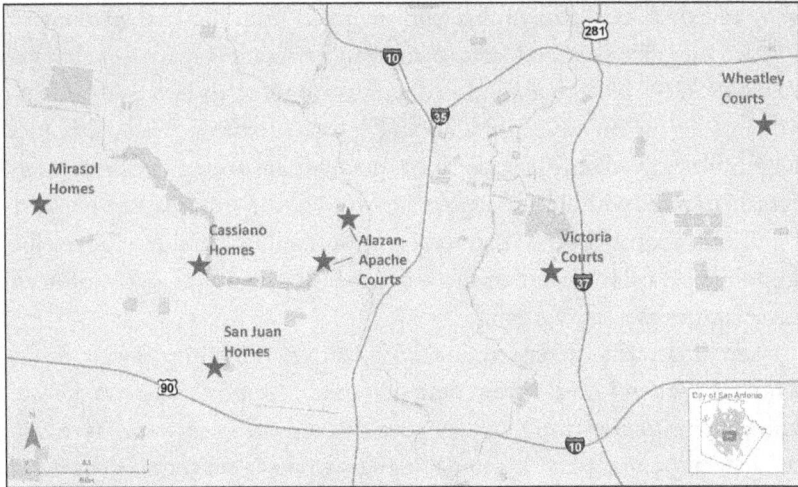

San Antonio Public Housing Courts, ca. 1950s. *Courtesy Sara Eaves, San Antonio Housing Authority, City of San Antonio.*

names, locations, etc., are important to the work for accuracy, recurrent themes, and verification of facts. The method used by the author to assess inclusion of a specific individual (whether by formal name, street name, or mere inference), is known as "saturation" (see Jacobs 2004). When in the course of the research, certain names, occurrences, or other elements are recurrent across different subject interviews, one concludes that these were key within the barrio network and its social milieu, or that they typified the local barrio dweller. By no means do the persons mentioned comprise an exhaustive list, and my self-imposed "ground rules" were not to harm anyone's reputation or misrepresent them. Only facts that are well-known about individuals, many of them verifiable in newspaper accounts or other public records, are included.

Unos de los Vatos mentados[45]

A well-known 1950s member of Alazan was Joe Lupe Ledesma, who was short in stature but formidable on the street scene, especially with a blade. At age eighteen he was arrested for assault to commit murder, along with an associate named Fernando "Payaso" Ortegón, who at the time lived near the Menchaca courts (*San Antonio Light* 1956 a). These arrests were part of an ongoing gang war between the Alazan and another West Side gang called El Alto. Part of this feud stemmed from the fatal stabbing of El Alto member George Garza at the San Fernando Gym (*San Antonio Light* 1956 b). Not long after, Ledesma is rumored to have stabbed another rival gang member at the Radio Club on Dolorosa Street, although he was never tried for that case. Such incidents are examples of meaningful occurrences within the barrio gang world of the era because they were significant acts of violence that took place at popular hangouts. Thus, Joe Lupe and his fellow members made a name for themselves and reinforced the Alazanes as a serious gang.

Ledesma was a career criminal with various stints in prison (a *pinto*) who was known for his threatening demeanor. Out on the street, he was known for *hikiando* (robbing) drug dealers, and there was a rumor that in the federal penitentiary, his unwillingness to pay a perceived debt owed to members of the New York Italian mob nearly resulted in a war between the Italians and the Chicanos from Texas ("Henry," The Boys Club). According to fellow members of Alazan, Joe Lupe exhibited several characteristics as a young adult that prevented him from making the transition into the class of *ruedas,* i.e., big time players or drug entrepreneurs. First, as his reputation was based on his use of the knife, many claim he was over-reliant on this means of protection or assault, and he therefore wasn't known to carry a gun. On one occasion, at the age of twenty-four, he did, however, get into a shootout with police (*San Antonio Express-News* 1963), but several subjects claim this was an anomaly. Secondly, and perhaps related to this perceived handicap, he never owned a car, making him susceptible to attack by a rival or contact with police. Lastly, and also related to these points, he was a known drug user, a known *boogla* (burglar), violence-prone, and therefore he had many enemies.

Ledesma was killed in 1981 at age forty-two in a well-known West Side bar called El Gallo Giro (Texas Department of Health 1981), known for many years prior as El Foro. It is rumored that he was killed by a former member of the barrio El Con.[46] A popular hangout for former barrio youth in the 1960s and 1970s, the bar was then run by Roy Mandujano, a once-convicted drug dealer (*San Antonio Express-News* 1973) and respected West Sider from the barrio known as la Guada. It was located on one of the West Side's most infamous avenues for vice, violence, and all things barrio-related: Guadalupe Street (Martinez 2014). It had numerous slang references including la Guada, el Weso, and la mera mata, and

is an inner-city avenue about three miles long, stretching from downtown (Flores Street) westward into Ghost Town turf toward las Colonias.
Today, the portion near downtown is nicely renovated, but after only a
few blocks west, it degrades to its previous state, a place where vice and
poverty remain rampant.

One of Joe Lupe's associates from Los Alazanes was Beto "El Borrado"
Guerra, who was one of four Guerra brothers from the courts, all of them
good fighters, buglas, etc.[47] One brother, Caetano, lost his arm to a Texas
prison guard's shotgun in a security mishap at the Harlem I state prison unit
that left another San Antonio inmate, Placido "Plastic" Villarreal of the Circle barrio, dead (*San Antonio Light* 1957 (f)). Another well-known member
of the courts, and longtime rival of Joe Lupe, was "Poninas" Sanchez (still
living), who was also claimed by the Boys Club, a very large barrio gang
whose turf was near downtown, in the Bounds. Poninas spent more of
his adult life in jail and prison than out on the street. He is also said to
have been one of the first youth to introduce *carga* (heroin) to the courts
in the early 1950s.

Juan "Ronia" was also from the courts and well known in the streets.
He was from a very poor family and was known as an old-school *pachuco*
(flashily dressed). His arms were covered in tattoos and he dressed in
white t-shirts, suspenders, pressed, pleated pants, and Stacies.[48] A pachuco's speech, dress, and mannerisms are similar to those of the zoot-suit or
cholo subculture that originated in East LA and El Paso, Texas, where the
slang argot known as *caló* is used, low-rider cars are driven, etc. (Moore
1978; Mirandé 1987; Vigil 1990). Since Juan Ronia was known most for
favoring that style, it is perhaps no surprise that he eventually moved to
California, where he died.[49]

There was a deadly family feud occurring throughout West Side San
Antonio barrios throughout the 1950s and 1960s involving a large family
from the Alazan courts. The Rubio brothers were Carlos, Henry, Lupe,
Poncho, and Chuy. Their rivals, the Mercados (Juan, Chano, Victor, Luis,
and Reyes [a cousin]) were said to be from the south end of the courts,
near an area known as La Tripa (Vera Cruz Street). While there were
several back-and-forth retaliation killings over the years, the only known
documented account of the origin of the feud appeared in a newspaper
statement given by a narcotics lieutenant of SAPD in 1959; it was described as a "two-year-long feud between [the families] who have warred

over dope-selling rights within a 4-block Westside area" (*San Antonio Light* 1959 b). By that point, there had been three back-and-forth killings, with the most recent being the murder of Carlos Rubio by Juan Mercado and his cousin Reyes Mercado (*San Antonio Express-News* 1958). Other than these newspaper accounts, little is known about the exact origins and details of the feud, except that it began as a "petty dispute in the shallow West Side streets of Chihuahua and San Jacinto" ("Lefty," Los Courts).

Henry Rubio, a career criminal and longtime *pinto*, was the last survivor of the Alazan-based Rubios. He also had ties to the barrio known as La Calle Austin on the East Side. He, too, played a role in the high-profile stabbing death of a rival at a bebop dance at the San Fernando Gym, as did "Richio" Garcia of the Courts, but neither was tried on the murder charge (*San Antonio Light* 1956 b). Unfortunately, Henry Rubio passed away just before this study began in 2012, taking with him many valuable firsthand accounts of various legendary incidents in San Antonio barrio and prison warfare.

Other *vatos mentados de los courts* include Mike "Curly" Carrillo (deceased), a known heroin dealer in his late teens (*San Antonio Express-News* 1958), and a bar owner in adulthood (1970s), who was once acquitted of murder but who did a brief stint in prison for drug trafficking. A one-time business partner of his, Juan "Chavalo" Ferrel (murdered, unsolved), was said to be the gang's leader in the 1950s. Juan Chavalo's brother Píle was also murdered because of narcotics-trade politics. Other notable 1950s era *soldados* from the Courts included "El Jiggies," "El Birdie" Sanchez (murdered), "El Kila" (Gonzales)[50], Abel "Yepo" Gil (deceased), Alex "Lefty" Fuentes (and nine siblings), "Nati" Lopez (deceased), brother "Pilinga," Gilbert Orozco, "El Panther," "El Sombra," "El Pepino," "Joka" (Lopez), [51] "Venena" Castro, "El Chimilio" Vasquez, "Capone" Apreciado, "El Private," and "Henry de la Madre," to name a few.

The Cassiano Courts

Of the seven other Chicano-based housing projects in San Antonio, the next most potent context for barrio gang processes over time has been the Cassiano Courts. According to an early 1980s US Housing and Urban Development Anti-Crime Program carried out in San Antonio (and fourteen other cities), the vicinity of the Cassiano homes had one of the highest crime rates in the city. It was even higher than the notorious San Juan homes, which were constructed two years before the Cassianos. The first four hundred housing units within the Cassiano Courts were built in 1953, with an additional ninety-nine units built in 1966 (San Antonio Housing Authority 2014). The 499 housing units accommodate some 2,200 residents on average. In 1980, 68 percent of the residents were seventeen years of age or younger, 71 percent of households were headed by a single parent, and rates of unemployment and welfare dependency were significantly higher than the city, state, and national rates (US Dept. of Housing and Urban Development 1984). These socioeconomic characteristics are still largely present today (US Census 2015 [a]).

One of the most notable physical features of the Cassiano homes are the 125 murals painted on the street-side units, each depicting some aspect of Mexican or Chicano history, culture, religion, or other aspect of social life for these populations.

Maize mural, Cassianos Courts. *Photo courtesy of Eddie "the Cruiser" Cruz.*

Religious mural, Cassianos Courts. *Photo courtesy of Eddie "the Cruiser" Cruz.*

The artwork was done by the Community Cultural Arts Organization in the 1970s as a pro-social outlet for area youth with after-school, weekend, and summer participation. Community organizers and youth met with older residents to hear stories of the area and gather ideas for murals (City of San Antonio 2014). Nonetheless, of the housing projects' atmosphere, the 1984 HUD report stated:

> Graffiti was ubiquitous, a trademark of the Cassiano Homes. Other highly visible forms of anti-social behavior associated with the project's large youthful population were truancy, systematic intimidation of families by older youth, and substance abuse, such as glue- and paint-sniffing (U.S. HUD 1984: 7).

The needs assessment for attracting anti-crime HUD funds to the Cassianos included feedback from its Resident Association, which reported their major crime-related concerns as vandalism, burglary, insufficient lighting, the need for a police presence, and a general sense of inadequate security. The funding application also listed the lack of organized, supervised recreation programs for youth, the high consumption of alcohol, and a lack of privacy resulting from population density. Like the Alazanes, the barrio gang associated with the Cassiano Courts simply identified themselves as being from the Cassianos, however, there were members of other gangs whose turf was nearby who hung out there, or who went in to score drugs. By the late 1980s, it was home to members of three of San Antonio's most active Chicano gangs, the BCs (Bad Company), 8-Ball Posse (a.k.a. *Puro Ocho*), and the LA Boyz (Sikes 1997).

A well-known member of the 1950s era Cassianos gang was Juan Terrazas, who was an ex-pinto who "always carried a *filero* (knife)" (interviewee #03). Jesse (Chuy) "Hamburger" Sanchez from the Cassianos was a heavy drug user and ex-pinto who was well known throughout various San Antonio barrios, and who spent much time in the Bounds. His nephew "Jira," of the Varsity Drive-In and Lake Gang areas, was more of a sidekick to him than his own brother Martin "Movie" Sanchez, another well-known barrio dweller nonetheless. When "Hippo" from Taco Village began his first sentence in state prison at Texas's Eastham unit, he credits Chuy Hamburger with having schooled him about prison culture in ways that probably saved his life.

Other well-known members of the 1950s era Cassiano Courts were "Chayio" and his brother, "El Professor," who lived by Cassiano Park. They were some of the first San Antonio barrio gang youth known to wear baggy pants (now endemic to this subculture), and who both eventually "did prison time" (were pintos). Another pair of brothers from the Cassianos were Nacho and Fabian Castillo, who also were ex-pintos. There were also Lupe "El Chicken" Barrera, "El Ponka," and "Lira," who was known to have nice cars and, as a result, lots of girlfriends. Little Joe Barrera were a reputable barrio youth from La Piedrera, but with close ties to the Cassianos. Paul Valdez, Chemo Ortiz, Avelardo, and El Apache were also known members from the 1950s-era Cassianos.

El Alto was a gang from a residential area adjacent to the Cassianos. Its leader in the 1950s was Rudy Gomez, who at age seventeen shot (at close range) two rival gang members from Ghost Town: Tony Pedraza and Pablo Montoya (*San Antonio Light*, 1957 d). Norberto "Congo" Soto (ex-pinto, still living) was another well-known member of El Alto who remained a member of the barrio criminal network well into adulthood as an associate of Martin Guerrero, whose story is told later in this chapter. In 1970, Congo was given a ten-year prison sentence for mere possession of narcotic paraphernalia (*San Antonio Light* 1970), which was not uncommon under the strict drug sentencing reforms initiated by US Senator Price Daniel (Texas) in the late 1950s. An infamous member of El Alto who often hung around the Cassianos was Arturo "El Joka" Alejandro. As a youth, he was one of numerous San Antonio barrio gang kids to be committed to the Gatesville State School for Boys. As a young adult, he gained notoriety for the string of armed robberies he committed around the city over several months in 1964. His signature modus operandi for these "stick-ups" was the use of a Halloween mask, earning him the nickname "The Halloween Bandit" in the press and in the community. He was eventually tried and convicted for the robberies (*San Antonio Light* 1964).

The San Juan Homes

For over five decades, the San Juan Homes were another of San Antonio's most potent contexts for barrio gang activity. Built in 1951, they sit only a few city blocks south of the Cassianos off a main thoroughfare, Zarzamora Street (See Figure 1 above). The housing project underwent several phases of construction, with a major addition in 1967 that expanded it to 458 public housing units on forty-one acres (San Antonio Housing Authority 2014). Redevelopment efforts in 2008 and 2010 began to move it away from its "public housing" identity. Its most recent renovation in 2014 transformed it into market-rate living for the new urban professional class that is gentrifying the neighborhood. This has also been the fate of a smaller housing project once adjacent to the San Juan Homes called the Brady Courts, now an upscale development called the Brady Gardens.

For over fifty years, Los San Juanes were the home base of Varrio La Blanca (VLB). The gang took its name from the *tiendita* called "La Blanca" on its turf. "La Blanca" was also the name of a nearby dancehall that held sock-hops for area barrio youth, to which VLB members were present with their *fileros* (blades) tucked away in case of any trouble with other barrios.[52] Although other gangs have dwelled within the San Juanes over the years, this original group, VLB, remained intact for five consecutive decades. As a multigenerational gang, it developed

San Juan Homes. *Photo Courtesy of the San Antonio Housing Authority.*

ties to prison gangs in the 1990s that became stronger over that decade. Valdez and colleagues (2004; 2005; 2009) reported on the general structure of the gang's drug-dealing operations from the late 1990s through the early 2000s, using the thinly veiled pseudonym *Varrio La Paloma* (VLP). Around this time, the group became one of the most active West Side street gangs involved in the drug trade and had branched out of the Courts into several barrios on the southwest periphery of the city. At this point, the gang had some one hundred core members and about eighty associates (Valdez & Sifaneck 2004).

One of La Blanca's original barrio gang members was Hector Cordova, a former *tecato* (addict) known also as a good fighter who, after being released from prison, ran a drug recovery program in the late 1960s. A former associate of the VLB in the mid-1950s claimed Cordova was one of the barrio's leaders (#03). Other well-known ex-pintos from La Blanca were Joe Gonzales, Richard Gallegos, Tommy Votion, "Lupillo," Billy McDonald, Fred "La Bruja" Castro and his younger brother, "Little Joe." Chele Hinojosa was a VLB member who did not live in the Courts but in a modest home nearby.

After a fifty-year history as one of San Antonio's most notorious groups, Varrio La Blanca dissipated in the early 2000s because of several factors. As described by Valdez (2005), the gang evolved into a rather large drug-distribution network and the incarceration binge resulting from the federal "War on Drugs" in the 1990s served to lock up many of its core members. As previously noted in this chapter, zero-tolerance policies of the San Antonio Housing Authority (SAHA) also augmented this process; thus the San Juan Homes were no longer the traditional home base of the VLB as they had been for so long. Valdez (2005) noted that higher-ranking members of the VLBs, their rivals, the LA Boyz, and other serious West Side Chicano gangs in the 1990s like the 8-Ball Posse from the Cassiano and Alazan Courts joined various prison gangs, leaving these street gangs to dissolve or morph into prison-street hybrid groups.

The Victoria Courts

The Victoria Courts were among the first housing projects built in San Antonio, shortly after construction of the Alazan-Apaches. It was a 660-unit development located in the inner-southeastern portion of the city near downtown until it was demolished in 1999. By the 1950s it had become inhabited by poor Mexican American families, primarily. Although many reputable barrio youth grew up in and around these courts, it was noted as former home to the most well-known local barrio-boy-turned-drug-kingpin to emerge from a San Antonio slum. Fred Gomez Carrasco's life is chronicled in *The Heroin Merchant,* written by former *San Antonio Express-News* writer Wilson McKinney (1975). Ben Olguin (2010) and David Montejano (2010) also wrote about Carrasco as a charismatic, intelligent Chicano who probably could have been extremely successful in the legitimate world.

Although Carrasco lived in the Victoria Courts in the 1950s, he is not among the more notable teenage barrio gang-youth personas of that era. One interviewee faintly recalls that he might have gone by the street name "Tuffy." Carrasco's first serious crime came at age eighteen, when he and an accomplice murdered a young man at a school dance on South Alamo Street, not far from the Victoria Courts (McKinney 1975). Carrasco was convicted and sent to prison for five years.

Like gangs from other housing projects, the barrio gang from the Victoria Courts identified as such, abbreviating the name to Los VCs.

One of the first notable heroin traffickers from the Victorias was Rudy Reyna, active in the late 1940s and early 50s, with ties to the infamous Georges brothers, known traffickers and operators of the Embassy Bar in downtown (*San Antonio Light*, 1957 (e)). Some of the well-known 1950s-era youth from this barrio were Richie "Dragnet" Cardenas, his brother Poncho, Buddy Torres, and Lucio Felix. "El Heavy" was well known in many barrios, and was claimed by both the VCs and the Boys Club in the Bounds. "El (E)Speck" was a well-known member of the VCs who was murdered by a rival gang. According to McKinney (1975), Tuffy's sidekicks in the Victoria Courts were "El Muerto" and "Angel," but this study did not unearth any such affiliates of the 1950s era VCs. In the 1980s and 1990s, the VCs were known as the Victoria Court Gangsters (VCGs), until word of the impending demolition of these projects began to spread, and families were relocated by the San Antonio Housing Authority (SAHA) to various other public housing and section-eight units around the city starting in 1999. Another longstanding contemporary Victoria Courts-based gang is "The Fellas," which formed in the 1980s and is thought to still be intact (see chapter 7).

Other West Side Housing Projects

Villa Veramendi

The Southmost of the Chicano-based housing projects was the Villa Veramendi Homes, a.k.a. "Los Veramendis." Situated between the quintessential West Side high school called Lanier and the Edgewood Independent School District boundary, it was one of the last of the West Side housing projects to be built, enrolling its first families in 1954. In the mid-1950s, its street-oriented resident youth were most likely to have joined Ghost Town or the Lake, who were the nearest, largest gangs to these projects at that time. The first distinct gang to emerge from the Veramendis was the Detroit Gang in the early 1960s (Montejano 2010; Valdez n.d.).

Lincoln Heights

On the periphery of the inner West Side housing projects were three remaining Chicano-based projects. To the northwest were the Lincoln Heights and the Menchaca Courts. These projects were constructed fourteen years apart, separated by a mile-long stretch of Poplar Street. Lincoln Heights was one of the first public housing projects to be built in San Antonio (1940), and was thus nearer to the inner city than the Mirasoles and Menchacas, both built in the mid-1950s. The "Lincolns" were about a mile east of the Menchacas, near Zarzamora Avenue, and near old barrios like the House of Neighborly Service, Los Luckeys (Lockett's corner store), and Espiga. Given that the Lincolns have always been a mixed-race housing facility (black and Latino), its 1940s and '50s street-oriented Chicano youth joined these longstanding barrio groups instead of starting a group specifically associated with the courts.[53]

Although it took four decades to formally develop, a mixed-race gang did eventually emerge from the Lincoln Courts. By the early 1990s, the Lincoln Court Kings (LCKs) were a very large and notorious gang in San Antonio. The gang eventually split into two groups, basically along racial-ethnic lines. While not strictly divided on this basis, the Kings were predominantly the Chicano faction and the Lincoln Court Gangsters (LCGs) were the black component of the Courts.

By 1999, gang issues in the Lincoln Courts became so pronounced that the district attorney was granted a civil gang injunction by the state attorney general. This was precipitated in part by the two main gangs colluding for drug distribution and other street crimes, making gang activity in this neighborhood among the most rampant and disruptive in the city. The injunction prohibited any member of the LCKs or LCGs to congregate in public, to possess alcohol or weapons (broadly construed), or to use cell phones in public. It placed strict curfews on group members and prohibited a number of other actions that essentially banished members of the groups from the premises. Patrol and gang officers were charged with enforcing the injunction and did so zealously, which suppressed gang activity there for several years. Ten years later, when old members began to parole and a new generation of gangsters came of age, a second injunction against these two gangs was issued (*San Antonio Express-News* 2009).

Menchaca Courts

The Menchacas were constructed in 1954, making it one of the more contemporary West Side housing projects. As in the Veramendis, which were also constructed in 1954, the street-oriented youth from these projects initially gravitated to the established groups in the area, such as the

Varsity Drive-in barrio. As they were also near the Lincoln Courts, they were likely to fall in with several of the groups available to those youth in the 1950s. Another large barrio on the outskirts of the West Side known as *Las Colonias* was also fairly accessible turf to Menchaca Court kids. "Lucio" was one of the well-known 1950s barrio youth uniquely from the Menchacas. More youth from the Menchacas made their mark in the 1960s than the 1950s.

The Mirasol Homes

The Chicano-based housing project located farthest from the inner city were the Mirasol homes, or *Los Mirasoles*. It was the west-most set of courts, situated a bit further out from Our Lady of the Lake University (See Figure 1 above). The impoverished neighborhoods surrounding the university's Elmendorf Lake were claimed by a gang called "the Lake." Los Mirasoles were situated between this barrio and Las Colonias. Built in 1953, Los Mirasoles began with 247 single-family homes, eventually growing to a 500-unit housing project (SAHA 2014). Montejano (2010) wrote about the status of this locale in the 1960s, listing the primary gang's name as "Mirasol"; but considering its placement within the city, it must have contained members of the Lake in the 1950s, which was a sizeable group. This housing project is still intact today, having been scaled down to 106 units in the early 2000s. Some of the well-known 1950s guys from the Mirasoles included "Chango" Armendariz, his brother Rudy, Fred Cruz, Rudy "El Chambon" Araiza, "Satanas," "El Cucaracho," "El Cuadrado," "El Copper," and "El Rainbow." A barrio police officer of that era, Bob "El Gordo" Cruz, was also from the Mirasoles.

The Barrio at Large

As critical as the various "courts" were in shaping the 1950s barrio gang scene in San Antonio, the dense web of connections between groups and individuals belonging to this subculture had a citywide reach. Barrio gang origins were depicted in chapter 2, but in somewhat general terms. This is because the role of past generations in shaping modern barrio network structures is in constant flux. Therefore, there are few clear starting points for describing key contexts outside of the Chicano housing projects and the Bounds. From these two areas, barrios tended to spring up in various parts of the inner city, and the associations between individual members of different gangs were rather fluid. Here again, two main criteria were used to select the examples I present for the citywide context. First, each was selected for its ability to help capture the essence of the barrio's delinquent subculture. Secondly, these are the elements (stories, names, etc.) that garnered the broadest consensus among subjects as to how they occurred; and/or they were documented in newsprint or other sources that supported the oral history narratives.

Los Patos

Jesse and Pete Gonzales were brothers who both went by "Pato" (duck) but who ran with different barrio groups. This arrangement was fairly common among brothers who were close in age. For example, "Hamburger" and "Movie" Sanchez, los Mantecas Rodriguez, Los Trampes Avila, Los Camarones, Los Supercats, and "Bunny" and Richie Lozano are all examples of well-known pairs of brothers who often hung out with separate barrio groups. In 1957, El Pato grande (i.e. the older brother, Jesse), then twenty years of age, was part of a group of seven youth from the south inner city barrio Taco Village (Nogalitos Street), who robbed, beat, and killed an elderly San Antonio attorney (*San Antonio Light* 1957 c). One of Pato's accomplices was Joe "Joka" Robledo (see endnote #51). Another defendant in that case who was eighteen at the time and a well-known barrio dweller is still alive today—Jose "Cote" Arias. El Pato Chico, then sixteen years of age, congregated with a younger cohort and was not part of this assault.

As for los Patos's citywide reputation, a *San Antonio Light* newspaper article about the large South Side gang, the Circle, mentioned that one of the group's marijuana connections was Pato, who sold it outside of a Guadalupe Street bakery (Schott 1958). This was clearly the younger Pato, Pete, and the location was most likely Los Cocos Bakery in the Bounds, as he was a known member of Los Cocos gang. In the photo below, El Pato chico (left) and Felix "*El Oso*" (bear) Spencer,[54] also of Los Cocos, are apprehended by Sgt. Leonard "Toto" Salas et al. of the SAPD Juvenile Bureau in 1956.

El Tigre

Richard "*El Tigre*" (tiger) Rivera was a known and feared barrio dweller in the Bounds in the early and mid 1950s. He was claimed by both

Juvenile marijuana arrest with Toto Salas. *Courtesy* San Antonio Express *Newspaper photo archives at UTSA's Institute of Texan Cultures.*

the West Side Bounds and Los Cocos. He was what youth from this era would refer to as a *"Búle"* /booleh/, described as being incredibly reckless; he always carried a knife, and was known for using it ruthlessly. He was sent to the Gatesville State School for Boys in 1954 at age fourteen for heroin possession. When he was released, he went on a violent spree, stabbing three youth on different occasions within the span of a week. He was finally caught for stabbing Thomas "Daddy-O" Garza of El Town gang inside the lobby of the Central Post Office downtown, nearly killing him. One of his prior stabbing victims was the well-known Polo "Rock-n-roll" Garcia, of the Columbus gang, whom he also put in the hospital for several days (*San Antonio Express-News*, 1956 b).

Martin Guerrero

Martin Guerrero was a member of the Riverside Gang as a youth, but he earned his major reputation at age twenty-three when he and an associate robbed and killed the manager of Centeno's market as he returned from the bank (Davenport 1965). Guerrero ran a bar called Riverside at the time, and used some of the loot to purchase items he needed for it. In state prison, he was said to be an agitator, calling for inmate riots and fasts (Interviewees #10 & #21). Guerrero was on parole after twelve years of a twenty-year sentence, and he continued to be a controversial figure out in the free world. A bar he owned in the 1970s and '80s called the "Fabulous 50's" had mural paintings of gangsters and other images that the community considered inappropriate, forcing their removal ("Dracula," Los Cocos). It included images of then-Mayor Lila Cockrell being menaced by men with daggers and Sheriff Copeland hanging from a noose ("Chota," Los Cocos).

In 1990 Guerrero was busted for cocaine trafficking and returned to prison, where he eventually died. Guerrero's family owned a small concrete company in the West Side; thus he may have been more middle class than most of his peers. Upon the 1990 arrest, police officials were quoted in the newspaper saying Guerrero was a "Westside character who aspired to be part of the bigtime . . . but who could not achieve that status." They went on to say he was "real flashy, with big diamond rings and gold chains," but in the end, was just a "flunky who was trying to impress people" (Crouse & Edwards 1990). Research subjects stated he often rode around town in a limousine with an entourage who sold drugs for him and served as bodyguards. Members of this entourage included other well-known former barrio youth: "Congo" Soto (still alive), Merciades Sustaita, "Big Bob" Ortegon, Bernabe Guzman, and a fellow known simply as "Cále." In prison, Arturo "Perro" Gomez (Los Luckeys) was an associate of Guerrero's and, according to some, a fellow agitator.[55] Despite his many detractors and critics, it is clear that Guerrero did make a name for himself, which is an important objective for many characters within the barrio subculture.

Cops & Robbers

Tony "Bear" Lomas, a.k.a. el barbero, and brother Pedro Lomas, a known bugla and car thief, were South Siders from the Circle gang who ran a barbershop on Frio Street in the Bounds. It was where the San Antonio municipal court and police central substation are currently situated. Associates of the Lomas brothers stated that although the place was a *conección*, frequented by prostitutes and other addicts, well-known narcotics officers such as Manuel Ortiz and Jack Westbrook used to get their hair cut there. This theme applies to various settings where both underworld types and police were known to congregate. The Red Rock bar in the Bounds (see chapter 2) was one such place where known criminals, street types, soldiers, and cops often kept the same company, going back to the late 1930s and early 1940s (*San Antonio Light* 1940).

There were places outside of the Bounds where this was also true. In one case in the mid-1970s, an off-duty Chicano detective shot a man who pulled a gun on a pool shark named Henry Villagran in the latter's Foxhole bar in the seedy stretch of Frio City Road on the city's West Side. Villagran did not escape another attempt on his life in 1979 when he was shot dead in another of his bars called The Stork Club (Texas Department of Health 1979), located in the deep West Side near Zarzamora and Guadalupe Street.

Two of the most respected detectives in the barrio were Joe and Jesse Garcia, twin brothers who grew up in the Alazan Courts. They embodied all of the classic attributes of barrio cops. That is, to be good at their job, they relied on their intimate knowledge of the barrio and its many outlaw characters, or at least they had this edge on cops who were not raised in the barrio.[56] They were known to hang out at places in the Bounds that were popular among many of the *ruedas* (high-profile, capable criminals), such as the bar of *Inez la Chueca* ("Crooked Inez") at Frio and Houston streets. Inez was one of San Antonio's last old-fashioned madams who operated a bar known for facilitating gambling and prostitution well into the 1960s. Another of these places, known more for its drug dealing, was Mela's on Laredo and Brazos Streets. Below I profile several 1940s and '50s ruedas that the Garcia twins and other known barrio detectives like Nacho Rosas and Frank Castillon would have congregated with in bars like Inez's and Mela's.

1940s and 1950s Ruedas

As a large Southwestern city with a vibrant red light district and a narcotics trafficking history, San Antonio has been the operating ground of a long list of Chicano outlaws going back to the 1920s, when the sale of heroin was made illegal in the United States. One of the oldest kingpin Chicano drug traffickers in San Antonio was Ventura Rodriguez, a.k.a. "Venture," who had an arrest record of narcotics possession going back to 1923 (Allen, 2009). Like the many San Antonio-based Chicano drug traffickers who would come after him, he served several sentences in federal prison—first for morphine, and then for heroin. Rodriguez was shot and killed in an exclusive basement bar in west downtown San Antonio in 1946 (Allen 2009).

Rodriguez's successors as Chicano kingpins in the 1940s would have included Hilario Medina, who was ten years senior to his brother Marcelino, a reputable early 1950s dealer. Agustin Moreno was another who was first busted for possessing significant amounts of heroin in 1946 and was a fourth-time narcotics offender by 1961 (*San Antonio Light* 1961). Police referred to David "La Rata" Vasquez as a "jewel" of a catch, who, at age thirty-seven, had been busted with heroin in Houston in 1952 before being busted again with the Georges brothers, well-known traffickers, in San Antonio in 1957 (*San Antonio Light* 1957-e). While a former member of the Courts, at the time of the bust, he lived in the inner South Side between the territory of longtime enemy gangs La Dot and El Circle.

One of the best-known traffickers of the 1940s, known by reputation and in some cases personally by the research subjects in the current study, was Mateas Martinez. His name seldom surfaced in newspaper archives, but he was referred to as "San Antonio's Dope King" in a 1954 article that also mentioned the arrest of known rueda Martin Cuellar (*San Antonio Express-News* 1954). Martinez was said to own the nicest Cadillac in the barrio and to be a flashy character. He told a (much younger) fellow federal inmate interviewed for this study that he'd once stood over a rival dealer, Andres "Bicicleta" Saldivar, with a pistol, attempting to shoot him, but he ran out of ammunition before he could strike the fast-moving Bicicleta, who was writhing on the ground dodging bullets! While Martinez lived to age ninety, passing away in a retirement home in 2005, Bicicleta, a World War II vet, a crane operator, bar owner, and tecato, died of lung cancer at age fifty-eight (Texas Department of Health 1980). Judging from the various newspaper archive stories detailing violent episodes involving El Bicicleta, he appeared to have lots of enemies, most of whom he got the upper hand on, including Joe Rodriguez, whose murder he was acquitted of on a self-defense argument (*San Antonio Light*, 1949-b).

Other 1940s and early 1950s ruedas that deserve mention are Fernando Rodriguez-Solsona, Lupe Rocha-Villarreal, Chuy Guerrero, Paulino Rangel, Simon Moreno, and Octiviano Gonzales, all of whom were named in early 1950s federal heroin cases appearing in newspaper archives and who were said to be repeat offenders. There was also a group of men who were not heroin dealers per se, but who were well known within the barrio street subculture for other exploits such as dealing in marijuana, pimping, or violence. Rudy "Boogie" Tamayo ran a shoeshine stand in the Bounds in the late 1940s and early 50s, was a tecato known for playing the piano in various bars and for dealing marijuana ("Bonne," Boys Club). Francisco de Soto was also a known marijuana dealer of the era (*San Antonio Express-News* 1952-b). Several 1940s *padrotes* (pimps and small-time drug dealers) operating in the various bars in the Bounds included "El Bigotes," "El Chapote," and Raymond "El Prieto." Some of the more dangerous men in their midst with long rap sheets for violence included Lencho Mascota, Margarito "Mague" Torres, and Tomas Sanchez, rumored to be a hit man for hire ("Nivo," Los Italianos). Torres stands out as an unruly and slippery character, often fleeing to Mexico after his violent actions in the Bounds landed him on local and state most-wanted lists. His outlaw status even had the attention of J. Edgar Hoover, then head of the FBI. Torres often eluded authorities by "laying low" in Nuevo Laredo while running a shoeshine stand and using the alias Santos Vasquez (*San Antonio Light*, 1942).

Summary

The delinquent intensity of 1950s barrio gangs was shown to be much higher than expected by casual observers of this era's street subcultures. To depict a rather violent 1950s barrio gang scene in San Antonio, this chapter profiled several of its key contexts and individual actors. This began with the government-subsidized housing projects, its resident gangs, and profiles of some of its most notable members. Several popular youth hangouts, other staging areas for gangs, and some of the incidents that helped to define violent conflict in the era were also detailed. The chapter illustrated the types of behaviors and characteristics of citywide barrio actors into early adulthood that cemented their reputations for the next few decades. Finally, the longevity of the street lifestyle and outlaw behavior as a constant feature of urban Chicano communities was shown with many of the known ruedas, or central figures in this atmosphere going back to the 1940s.

Barrio Maturation

The last few chapters defined the barrio's broader parameters, profiling some of the characters who operated within it, and demonstrating both the typical features they shared and their idiosyncrasies. Chapter 5 traces developments in this subculture over the next several decades and its network implications within an intensifying drug scene. In this context, the early to mid-1970s was known locally as the "Fred Carrasco era." Carrasco was perhaps the most notable kingpin to emerge from San Antonio's barrios (McKinney 1975). He employed many San Antonio barrio youth, a fact that is barely recognized in prior works on his life, but it is common knowledge among the persons interviewed in this study. McKinney's (1975) work on this era presented a unique take (often through the lens of Detective Bill Weilbacher), and didn't quite chronicle the barrio connections to fully illustrate the importance of the street to higher-level operations across generations. The next chapter therefore defines the barrio network structure that preceded and enabled a character like Carrasco to emerge. This timeline provides a bridge to the prison gang era's dominance of the heroin trade detailed in chapter 6.

Five

The Barrio Landscape Expands:
the 1960s and 1970s

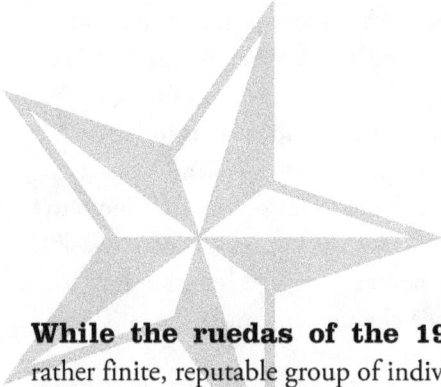

While the ruedas of the 1940s and early '50s were a rather finite, reputable group of individuals, the number of rungs in the drug-trafficking hierarchy quickly expanded in subsequent years, with many lower and mid-level dealers emerging in the growing city. If drug trafficking, substance abuse, and addiction were salient aspects of barrio life in the 1940s and 1950s, they were ever more prominent in the 1960s and '70s, propelling the state's incarceration binge. For lots of 1950s barrio youth, their street gang networks uniquely positioned them to engage in higher-order barrio activities as young adults, especially of the illegal and quasi-legal sort. This chapter begins by addressing the local *cantina* as a key context for these facets of barrio life, and advances the timeline in the local story of drugs and violence in the barrio.

Bars in the Bounds and in the shallow West Side are a historical nexus for barrio youth. While bars are generally adult venues, their abundance in these areas of the city in the 1940s and '50s made them a draw for local youth, who flocked to them to watch wrestling matches and other attractions on television (*San Antonio Light* 1951). The shoeshine stands in the area, which many barrio youth worked in, congregated in, and formed street corner societies in during the 1920s and 30s (Casillas 1994) had a bar-like atmosphere, with pool tables, jukeboxes, marijuana and cigarette smoke in the air, and so on. Going back as far as the 1880s, youth served as "messenger boys" in the red-light district's "cribs," i.e. brothel-bars (Bowser 2003; Sanders 2014). Streetwise youth have thus been part of the inner city's bar landscape for some time.

On Bars and Bar Owners

The numerous bars, taverns, and dance clubs in San Antonio's central districts were settings for much barrio networking activity, both legal and illegal. Barrio bars are not just networking mechanisms for crime-involved dwellers; managing such a bar is a viable occupation for many streetwise Chicanos looking to support themselves in a manner consistent with their lifestyles and reputations as tough guys, wise guys, or both. Indeed, several reputable individuals in the 1950s barrio gang scene later opened up bars named after the "owner's"[57] boyhood gang. Recall, for example, the account of Martin Guerrero's Riverside bar, located in that barrio's turf, in chapter 4. There was also the legendary Los Cocos Lounge, named after the longstanding barrio of Los Cocos in the Bounds (see chapter 2), run by Juan "Chota" Mendoza (still living).[58]

One's reputation in the barrio youth scene determined the odds of running a successful bar in the central city or in the infamous West Side. That is, being a known, *respected* person in the barrio was good for the bar's reputation, and thus for business. The way one won respect within the San Antonio youth barrio subculture in the 1950s was essentially by being a good fighter, by being loyal to one's barrio, being trustworthy (not a *relaje* [snitch]), and for generally embodying the traditional Chicano streetwise ideal of machismo (Casillas, 1994; Montejano 2010). Recall, from chapter 4, for example, that while "membership" into a barrio was loosely defined, adherence to the general street code was paramount in determining one's ability to remain in the company of ignoble characters. As a practical matter, running a barrio bar is a tough business because of the lawless and rowdy nature of many of its patrons. The owner must be able to hold his (or her) own in any situation where patrons attempt to intimidate, extort, or generally cause trouble by fighting or being unruly in the bar.[59]

As a generic context, the *cantina* is an important setting to analyze barrio networks and activity in any particular timeframe. Its purpose as a socializing venue is a given, but the barrio bar per se, that is, the bar located in the barrio and/or whose clientele are primarily barrio dwellers, represents much more to this underworld. It serves as a venue for drug dealing, gambling, violence, and prostitution. It is also a place to celebrate one's criminal exploits by spending money after a successful business deal or other lucrative (trans)action, or for a rueda to flaunt a steady stream of income from such activity.

Because many police detectives recognized these dynamics, they regularly frequented some of the key places to try to get information for their investigations. On one occasion, an undercover federal narcotics agent named Louis Cerda was "made" by a group of Chicano wiseguys at Mela's bar in the shallow West Side. The ringleader, "Raton" Longoria (of the Boys Club barrio) assaulted the agent as the others robbed him of his weapon and cash (San Antonio Express-News 1959). Although the agent's undercover status was revealed, the investigation netted a group of mid-to-high level drug traffickers who were once active in barrio youth gangs. These included Gino Velasquez (Los Cocos), "Little Joe" Barrera (La Piedrera/Cassianos), Raymond de la Cerda (La Tripa), and Chuy Guerra (Alazan), among several others.

Given that the western portion of downtown once known as the Bounds comprised San Antonio's red-light district through at least the 1940s, bars and taverns were ubiquitous throughout this area well through the 1970s. Table 2 contains a list of many reputable barrio bars, indicates who their owner-operators were (where known), and supplies details of their significance within the barrio network. While there were far too many bars and taverns to comprehensively document, these represent a broad sampling of the typical linkages and dynamics associated with such places.

As is evident in the literature, and in portions of Table 2, bars in Latino barrios are magnets for violence and homicide (Martinez 2014). One case making the newspaper in 1962 occurred at the renowned Stanley's Ice House on the West Side's main drag, Guadalupe Street, involving several barrio youth and a reputable narcotics detective named Curtis Creed. Creed and several patrolmen "happened to be passing by" the place, a regular hangout for barrio gang members, when a brawl broke out between eight to ten patrons, most of them teenagers (San Antonio Light 1962). Among the more reputable vatos arrested for assault and drug possession were Joe Lupe Ledesma of the Alazan Courts, Pablo "Little Pále" Esquivel (La Tripa/Alazan), and Lucas "McCain" Rodriguez Jr. (La Piedrera). As noted in chapter 4, Ledesma would be murdered by another former gang youth some twenty years later in El Gallo Giro, a bar a few blocks down on Guadalupe Street from Stanley's Ice House (Texas Department of Health 1981).[60]

Table 2: Sample of San Antonio Barrio Bars, Details, and Their Significance, 1940s – 1990s.

Bar	Owner–operator(s)	Location	Notes
La Fortuna (1960s – 1990s)	"Marcelo"	Bounds: Pecos & Guadalupe Streets.	A 1960s–90s *conneccion*. "El Ormiga" from the Wesley gang sold drugs there until the 1990s. Herb Huerta, future president of the Texas Mexican Mafia, was a bar regular. The owner was shot & killed there in the 1980s.
Quinto—Patio (1930s – 1960s)	"Pancho"	Bounds: by the historic *Alameda* theater	Reputable 1940s ruedas Joe Palafox & Jerry Valdez were regulars.
Moonglow (1930s – 1990s)	Harry Martinez in the 1970s and '80s.	Bounds: by the *Quinto Patio* bar	The barrio gang El Moonglow identified with this place from the 1930s through early 1950s.
The 1—2—3 Bar (1940s – 1970s)	Unknown	Bounds: Frio & Commerce Streets.	Near the Commerce Street bridge, a long-time drug *conneccion*.
Texas Inn (1940s – 1960s)	The Mendezes	Bounds: Frio & El Paso Streets.	El Farolito Night Club was upstairs from the bar. It was a 1950s barrio youth hangout.
Inez's (1940s – 1970s)	Inez "la Chueca"	Bounds: Frio Street & Buena Vista Avenue.	A place for gambling and prostitution; many off-duty cops also hung out there.
Reno Bar (1940s – 1970s)	Los "Italianos" Morelli in the 1960s and '70s.	Bounds: Monterrey & Pecos Streets.	Similar atmosphere to Inez's.

Red-Light Shoeshine (1930s – 1960s)	Rudy Tamayo	Bounds: Santa Rosa & Monterrey Streets.	Open-air shoeshine stand where 1950s barrio youth congregated, postured, and fought.
Monterrey (1950s)	Fred Carrasco, Sr.	Next door to the *Red-Light Shoeshine Stand*	San Antonio's most infamous drug kingpin from the barrio (Fred Carrasco) was the operator's son.
Berta's (1950s – 1970s)	"Berta"	West Side: Guadalupe & Nueces Streets.	Tomas "El Tacuache" Perales Sr. worked there. His son "Chacho" was a member of the nearby Los Cocos Gang.
Three Kings (1950s – 1960s)	Joe "Rayo" Villanueva & Mariano Gonzales	Conchos & Monterey St.	This was an old drug & prostitute *conneccion*. It was one of Fred Carrasco's hangouts.
Múcura (1940s – 1970)	Officer Manny Loredo	Bounds: Conchos Street.	Lots of violent episodes. Regulars were "El Bigotes" and "El Chapote," who worked for 1940s kingpin Mateas Martinez.
Sapo's (1970s – 1980s)	Officer Manny Loredo	Bounds: Conchos Street.	Loredo was Joe Lupe Ledesma's father-in-law (see chapter 4).
Atlas (1940s – 1980s)	Nacho de la Rosa	Bounds: Santa Rosa & Matamoros Streets. Later moved a few streets south, then to the *Cattleman's Square*.	Owner cashed checks, had a tiendita and pawnshop. Always had cash, "never got robbed." The bar never had female employees.
Red Rock (1930s – 1960s)	Los "Italianos", Morelli Brothers.	Bounds: Conchos & Matamoros Streets.	The bar was a magnet for vice; off-duty officers hung out there.

continued

Bar	Owner–operator(s)	Location	Notes
El Palmiero (1940s – 1970)	Pete Carreon	Bounds: Laredo & Guadalupe Streets until the 1960s, then moved a few blocks south to S. Flores & Rische.	1950s barrio youth hangout. "La Bruja" (Varrio La Blanca) slashed "El Pato" (grande)(Los Cocos) there in the early 1960s.
Quarterback Lounge / CNR Lounge / Irma's (1960s – 70)	Lanier High School's former Quarterback / Ramon "Mon" Quintanilla & Carlos Perreira / Pete Torres	Bounds: Guenther & Flores Streets.	"Mon" was from Barrio *El Con* (see chapter 4). Carlos Perreira was brother of "Manotas" (still alive), who ran with the Blackjacks barrio.
Los Cocos (1980s – 2013)	Juan "Chota" Mendoza of *Los Cocos* barrio gang.	Bounds: Guadalupe & Flores Streets.	Walls were covered with photos & memorabilia of the barrio. Moved to South Side late 1990s.
Club Royal (1950s – 1970s)	Bob "El Gordo" (an anglo). Later, *El Siete* (Lake) ran it.	Downtown: Flores Street & Houston Avenue.	Hot spot for drug trafficking; violence. On separate occasions, Pete "Birdie" Sanchez, Joe Alaniz, and Jimmy Castillo were among those killed there.
Mela's (1930s – 1970s)	"Mela"	Inner West Side: Laredo & Brazos Streets.	A hangout for Chicano wise guys the Eguia–Baker brothers, the Rubio brothers, and numerous others. Details in this chapter.

Las Trancas (1950s – 1980s)	"Santos"	West Side: Guadalupe Street.	Bar in the heart of the West Side (Guadalupe St.) near all of the other historically violent places (see Martinez 2014). Now called "Cheers."
El Chemigo (1950s)	Lalo Donel	West Side: Guadalupe and Nueces Streets.	Known as a drug *conneccion*. Crespin Donel (Lato's son) was a member of the Ghost Town gang.
Gemini (1980s – 1990s)	Unknown	West Side: Guadalupe and Trinidad Streets.	On separate occasions, "Booger Ray" Mercado and "Scoobie" Cortinas were murdered there in the 1990s.
El Gallo Giro (1950s – 1960s)	Roy Mandujano	West Side: Guadalupe St.	In the 1970s the bar's name changed to El Foro; It remained a hotspot for drugs and violence.
El Coquito (1960s – 1970s)	Ferrel brothers	West Side: El Paso & Colorado Avenue.	Ferrel brothers (Alazan); drug traffickers as young adults; 2 of 3 murdered by other traffickers, 1970s.
El Gaucho (1940s – 1960s)	Rocha Brothers	West Side: El Paso & Navidad St.	Barrio gang: "El Gaucho," 1950s.
La Paloma (1960s – 1970s)	Ernestine & Melchor de los Santos, and Rudy Melendez	West Side: 1907 Guadalupe Street.	Owner was sister to Melchor de los Santos, leader of an infamous drug gang in the 1960s. Melchor gunned down two men there in 1964 "for making threats." (*San Antonio Express-News* 1964).

continued

Bar	Owner–operator(s)	Location	Notes
Blue Room Lounge (1970s)	Jesse "El Chalape" Santoy	Downtown West	"El Chalape" had international drug connections. He was Fred Carrasco's older cousin, who brought Carrasco into the business. More details in this chapter.
Tompay (1950–1980s)	"Simona"	Inner West Side: meatpacking sector, Laredo & Brazos Streets.	Bar was in barrio La Tripa; frequented by youth working in the meat-processing district. They carried around leather holsters ("vauchas") for meat-cutting knives, which were often used in bar fights, hence, *tripas* (guts).
Packer's (1950s–1980s)	"Chale"	Inner West Side; meatpacking sector, Brazos & Jean Streets.	Barrio La Tripa.
Riverside Bar (1960s)	Martin Guerrero	North Bounds: N. Frio Street & N. Laredo Avenue.	In the 1980s Guerrero ran the Red Rock bar & Fab 50s on far West Side. Both on Culebra Avenue.
La Cama (1960s)	Officer Ruben Rodriguez	Inner South: S. Presa Avenue.	Later, Rodriguez ran the *International Bar* in the Bounds.
The Sailboat (1950s–1960s)	Vicho Gomez-Ybarbo	Inner South (Barrio La Dot): Probandt Street.	Vicho (La Dot) was as associate of the Fred Carrasco clan.
The Grapevine (1960s–1970s)	"Shorty" & Son: Vicho Gomez-Ybarbo	Inner South (La Dot): Mitchell Street.	Shorty Gomez, Vicho's father, originally came from Wilson County, Texas.

Triangle (1970s)	Run by the Padrino of Herbie Huerta (Mexican Mafia President).	West Side: Frio City Road.	Chendo Gonzales (Los Cocos, see chapter 4) was shot there; survived, got clean and became a drug counselor at the Patrician Movement. The bar's owner was killed in the bar by his girlfriend.
The Stork Club (1970s)	Henry Villagran	Zarzamora & Guadalupe streets.	Owned by Henry Villagran. See chapter 4 for details about his death in that bar.
El Conquistador (Early 1970s)	Dan "Dandy" Berlanga & Jesse "El Chalape" Santoy.	West Side: Morales & Colorado streets.	Dandy (The Lake) was a high-level trafficker with the Fred Carrasco group (McKinney 1975). The bar was frequented by transsexuals before it became Dandy's.
Mike's Tavern (1990s – 2000s)	"Mike"	Far West Side: Culebra Avenue.	A popular Mexican Mafia hangout in the 1990s.
El Cometa (1950s – 1960s)	Unknown	Deep West Side: Gen. McMullen Street.	A hangout for the Cassiano and Mirasoles courts and other groups from Las Colonias.
El Jorongo (1980s)	Montemayor & "Sandy"	South Side: New Laredo Highway.	Strip Club. Now called "Secrets."
Ruby's Lounge (1970s)	Ruby Sanchez	Southwest Side, S. Gen. McMullen Street	Ruby was an operative in the Carrasco Organization
El Cuartel (1980s)	Mike "Curly" Carrillo	Far South Side: Somerset Road.	Carrillo (Calle Guadalupe) became a high—level drug trafficker.

continued

Bar	Owner–operator(s)	Location	Notes
La Escondida (1970s)	Montemayor & Sandy	South Side: New Laredo Highway.	Site of a major drug bust involving Fred Carrasco's people.
"Mike's" (1980s)	Carlos "Uncs" Alva	East Side: MLK Blvd., across from St. Phillip's College.	Carlos (The Circle) spent much of his adult life in prison for homicide and other crimes.
"Right on Jimmy" (1980s)	Lupillo Hernandez	East Side: Clark & Porter Avenue.	Lupillo, still living, (The Circle) remained active in barrio activity well into late adulthood.
The Cave (1960s – 1970s)	"Mayo" (Morales)	East Side: *Calle* Austin (Street).	A hangout of Rolle and Robe Salinas, Luz "Big Light," and Chuy "Muletas" Onofre (the latter still living).
The Mexican Hut (1960s – 1970s)	Unknown	East Side: *Calle* Austin (Street).	Similar profile to "The Cave."
Chicano Magic (1980s – 1990s)	Fernando Martinez	East Side: Clark Street.	In the early 1990s, the owner killed an unruly patron who pulled a knife.

A shootout at Gil's Place in the deep West Side (Zarzamora and Saltillo Streets) in 1970 killed three and injured three (*San Antonio Express-News* 1970). Interview data from a research subject (among others) who worked there at the time revealed that it was a group of the Carrasco clan's *pistoleros* who shot up the place over a personal dispute with the owner and some of the staff. Although never prosecuted for it, Joe Frank "El Diente" Perez and Jose Ramiro Silva, both formerly of the West Side's Melchor de los Santos drug gang, were rumored to be among the group of men who did the shooting. This shootout was an example of a new era of growing ruthlessness in carrying out operations, or as in this case, even in run-of-the-mill disputes in personal business.

Of the brand of street crime seen in San Antonio through the early 1960s, McKinney (1975: 13) wrote that the city was "accustomed at worst to the violence of the juvenile street gangs and Saturday night barroom brawls." The late 1960s and early 1970s, however, ushered in a new generation of extreme tactics to accompany the higher volume of drug trafficking, and thus higher stakes in that business. This period is commonly known as the "Carrasco era," as this group in particular seemed to set a new standard for drug-related violence in its operations that many feared and that future generations would follow. Indeed, there are several places in McKinney's work where the Carrasco group is referred to as "the Mexican Mafia" by keen observers, lawmen, and even in a *narco-corrido* written about the group by Daniel Garcez in 1973.

Before and Beyond *The Heroin Merchant*

In 1975, a small press called Heidelberg Publishers in Austin, Texas, published *Fred Carrasco: The Heroin Merchant* by Wilson McKinney, a *San Antonio Express-News* journalist. It was a detailed documentary of the criminal career of a San Antonio barrio native turned drug kingpin. No other work before or since has impressed the region's crime-intrigued public like this book did, a favorite among barrio residents, criminals, and crime fighters especially. Yet, for all that this groundbreaking book did to cement the legendary status of Fred Carrasco, as a socio-historical analysis, the work lacks context. To be fair, some background of the role of the Bounds in the heroin trade is offered, and the barrio roots of Carrasco and two other central characters, Frank "El Diente" Perez and

Tony de la Garza, are touched upon. However, although it immortalized Carrasco in San Antonio and the south Texas region, it barely scratches the surface of the barrio context that produced such a figure. It is therefore important to offer a more complete analysis of the drug scene, the players, and the cultural context Carrasco was influenced by.

In this regard, *The Heroin Merchant* goes only as far back as the days of the West Side's Melchor de los Santos drug gang, whose prime was in the early and mid 1960s, and who employed Carrasco and several other operatives from that era that were highlighted in the book. Furthermore, because it was a quickly written snippet (true to the style of McKinney's journalistic trade) it does not move beyond Carrasco in the timeline of narcotics trafficking and related barrio drama in San Antonio. Finally, the work relies much on the police perspectives of Bill Weilbacher, Manuel Ortiz, Dave Flores, and others from their cohort. In fact, "Big Bill" (Weilbacher) practically shared the spotlight with Carrasco as the main character in McKinney's work. This work builds around McKinney (1975) in all of these respects, describing the substratum of dealers and users that supported the higher-level operations of the Carrasco clan in San Antonio. Continuing along the timeline established in previous chapters, I document the patchwork of late 1950s dealers, which by then were better categorized as quasi-ruedas and small-time user-dealers who were well known in the barrio.

Quasi-Ruedas: The New Generation

According to police, in the late 1950s a younger, larger group of marijuana and heroin dealers began to replace a prior cohort of kingpins who had left town or were serving time in the penitentiary (*San Antonio Express-News* 1954; *San Antonio Light* 1958). A major roundup in October 1958 resulted from the issuance of thirty-five arrest warrants on twenty-one persons secretly indicted on narcotics charges. The average age of those arrested was twenty-two years (*San Antonio Light* 1958). The roundup was the culmination of months of undercover work by rookie officer Antonio Flores, a twenty-six-year-old Chicano. Some of the young hustlers with barrio reputations who continued on in drug trafficking after this bust were Rudy "El Morado" Davila (Boys Club), Eddie "Lil Bit" Espinoza (Boys Club), Mike "Curly" Carrillo (Calle Guadalupe), and Charlie "Joka" Guzman (Bounds/Red Light). There was a sizeable group operating in this timeframe who managed to go undetected by police for a longer period than those aggressive dealers identified and rounded up in this particular dragnet. Among them were brothers Joe and Jacinto "Chito" Baker, Luis "El Galleta" Hernandez, Raul "Manotas" Perreira (still alive), Raul "Ormiga" Solis, "Meme" Ortega, "Chóre" (i.e. "Shorty") Hamilton, Beto Montes, "El Cucaracho" Martinez (still alive), "Lito" Garza, Tony "El Trece" Melchor, Eloy Perez, Narcisso "The Nurse" Serna, "El Pano," Raymond "Scorpion" Sorder, the "Supercat" brothers, Henry Barron, Rudy Noria, the Sampayo brothers, and Willie "Mo" Moreno, to name a few. Like the previous list of ruedas, all of these men were from different groups in the Bounds and the Near West Side.

Recall that chapter 4 also profiled a great many reputable barrio youth. With only a few exceptions, this is also part of the group who were older than Fred Carrasco and who preceded him in the realm of street-level narcotics sales. Unless noted as 1940s ruedas, most of those were low- to mid-level dealer-users with deep roots in 1950s barrio gangs. Naturally, a few from this milieu rose to become higher-level dealers, and some of these were recognized as such in *The Heroin Merchant*. One of these was Daniel "Dandy" Berlanga, of the Lake gang in the 1950s, who played a major role in the de los Santos drug ring and later in Fred Carrasco's group. Dandy had six brothers, five of whom were Lake gang members who supported his movement into the class of ruedas by assisting in street level dissemination and sales. This bunch was allied with the man who is credited with bringing Fred Carrasco into the fold. This was Fred's older cousin Jesse "El Chalape" Santoy, who also gets lots of coverage in McKinney's book, but those who comprised the barrio network that distributed the large quantities he dealt in did not.

The exclusive focus on Fred Carrasco and those in his immediate circle kept McKinney from noting the barrio network in place to support these ruedas. Yet this street network is critical to the success (or failure) of the overall operation. There were also important details missed in the *Heroin Merchant* about players higher up the chain in the Santoy and Carrasco clans. An individual known throughout San Antonio's barrio and gentry circles alike is a player whom I will refer to as "the Godfather," his street name. "The Godfather" was perhaps known more for his efforts in legitimate business, Latino community outreach, and advocacy, than for his role in facilitating Santoy's rise to international drug-dealer status. There are at least three possibilities (hypotheses) for McKinney's failure to mention "the Godfather" in *The Heroin Merchant*. He might have been intentionally omitted because of his positive reputation in the community and lack of an arrest record. Alternatively, McKinney may not have known about his role as a financier, despite the fact that dozens, if not hundreds of others within the barrio network did. If that is the case, it reflects the limitations of McKinney's perspective—his reliance on police and public records information rather than information from barrio dwellers. A final possibility is that McKinney was discouraged from including the Godfather's name by members of San Antonio's power elite, of which the Godfather, a wealthy business owner, was a part.

With regard to street-level operations, *The Heroin Merchant* sidesteps the importance of barrio actors to the success of the higher-order drug operation that *was* highlighted. One example of this comes early in the book, regarding a bust involving *El Chalape* (Santoy) and his right hand, Dandy Berlanga. Although omitted by McKinney, involved in that bust were individuals that this study recognizes as being associated with the South Side's largest gang of the era, The Circle (*San Antonio Light* 1961 (a)). My findings suggest that the South Side barrio gang structure was a key part of the heroin distribution and street sales for the ruedas. Another example is in one of the central dramas in McKinney (1975) involving Daniel Jaramillo, who was both Carrasco's "base operations officer" (222) and a pawn in his revenge game against the detectives who pursued him. In the midst of the media frenzy surrounding the latter, Jaramillo and four other men were arrested with several pounds of heroin while Carrasco was awaiting trial for murder (*San Antonio Light* 1974). Among those arrested were individuals this study noted were members of the street gang La Dot, again suggesting that the South Side barrio structure was important to the organization's street operations.[61] In this case it was to its detriment, perhaps because of the inexperience of Jaramillo (twenty-six years old at the time) and his young associates.

The Growing City, The Growing Barrio

Between 1950 and 1960, the population of San Antonio (Bexar County) grew by 27 percent, from 500,460 to 687,151, and it grew another 17 percent over the next decade (US Census, 2015 (b)). A disproportionate amount of this growth was among the Chicano population, which has steadily become a larger portion of the county's residents over time (US Census, 2014). As the socioeconomic status of this group remains stagnant at best (Grogger and Trejo 2002; Murdock et al. 2013) this amounts to barrio expansion during the era. This has direct implications for the size and number of barrio gangs that would emerge during this time. As discussed by Montejano (2010), there was an explosion of barrio gang activity in San Antonio after 1960.

While several groups from the 1940s and '50s remained intact, increasing the size of their membership with new cohorts during the 1960s (e.g. La Blanca, Riverside, Varrio Grey Eagle), most of the original Chicano gangs of the Bounds became extinct when their neighborhoods were redeveloped. In terms of network implications, until this point in the barrio's history, proven, reputable barrio youth were a finite group, and as earlier chapters suggested, "everybody knew everybody." This made it possible for me to study that group's network properties descriptively. Even at that, I had to rely on less precise data when attempting to identify all of the members of groups to the far south (e.g. Varrio Palo Alto) or north of the city (e.g. Kenwood, Rattlesnake Hill). Not without its limitations for the 1940s and '50s, the peer-nomination method used to study the barrio gang universe clearly starts to become implausible from the 1960s onward because of the sheer growth in numbers of youth involved in the subculture (Montejano 2010).

The expansion of barrio conditions and populations into areas of the city that were new or previously uninhabited by Chicanos resulted in several shifts in networking dynamics. Recall, for example, from chapter 3 that most of the men from 1950s gangs interviewed for this study did not recognize many of the names of 1960s West Side barrio gangs profiled in 2010 by Montejano. Just as the number of barrio gangs grew in this era, so did the number of drug users, user-dealers, and quasi-ruedas. Drug use was declared an epidemic by politicians like Price Daniel, a Texas attorney general, then a US senator, and finally, governor of the state from 1957 to 1963. While a senator, his work on the Judiciary Committee resulted in recommendations on the problem of drug addiction and on changes to the Federal Criminal Code to address organized crime. These efforts trickled down to affect law-enforcement policies and tactics in San Antonio to combat the issue.

As the demand for drugs began to soar in the barrio, naturally the number of kingpins and their organizations began to grow. McKinney (1975) noted that by 1972, narcotics investigators accounted for nine

separate drug-trafficking rings in San Antonio with ties to Mexican suppliers. Some ten years prior, there were perhaps only five or six of these
groups, including that of Melchor de los Santos, the Georges Brothers, El
Chalape, and a few other ruedas from the 1940s and '50s who were still
in the business. Fred Carrasco's drug ring would become by far the most
successful, if not the most reputable of the San Antonio-based groups
operating in the early 1970s. He had a particular style of governance
that his Mexican operatives both feared and at times found peculiar, as
members were required to take a sworn oath of allegiance to the group
(under veiled and direct threats from Fred). These typically occurred at
critical points in their smuggling maneuvers when the stakes were high
(McKinney 1975).

The high-intensity level Carrasco employed in running his organization seems to stem, in part, from the cultural and economic contexts
that produced him. To begin, although he didn't directly participate in
barrio gang warfare, he grew up in that environment, was certainly from
those neighborhoods most affected, and was known and respected by
barrio gang youth. While seemingly more independent-minded than the
barrio youth who fell in with their respective groups, he proved to be
violence-prone as a very young man, picking up a murder charge at age
eighteen (McKinney 1975). He was not known to be a drug user himself, which also set him apart from many typical barrio youth. Lastly, as
the demand for drugs in the barrio was rapidly increasing when he was
released from prison in the early 1960s, the economic incentive, the timing, and his connection to El Chalape created the ideal conditions for his
rise to power.

Predecessors, Pioneers, and the Age-old *Reláje*

One of the key mechanisms used by Carrasco to set him and his group
apart from most others involved in the drug trade was intimidation on
the street and the ruthless use of violence within the organization. The
common refrain heard among my research subjects on this topic was
"Fred wanted to control everything." One interviewee stated, "If you
were scoring [dope] from someone besides Fred, and he found out about
it, he came to your place and threatened you" (Erasmo, Calle Guadalupe). Carrasco's operation became notorious in San Antonio rather
quickly because it was known to eliminate members of its own group for

perceived treachery. These tactics alarmed the public and politicians of the era, who viewed it as a new breed of gangsterism in the region that sought to emulate the Italian mafia. Ironically, Carrasco himself got his start by implicating his cousin El Chalape as being the "big man" in San Antonio's narcotics operations—part of a plea bargain when Carrasco was arrested by federal agents in 1961 (McKinney 1975).

The "rat" or the "snitch" is called a reláje in the barrio street subcultures of Texas. This form of self-interest or self-preservation as a part of human nature is perhaps timeless, or at least as old as organized justice systems around the world. As despised a status as it is in the barrio underworld and in prison, there is no shortage of relájes. It is an inherent and vital piece of the US criminal justice system, tying police investigations to prosecutorial decisions and ultimately to the courts through endless feedback loops. Snitching, or providing information about the activities of a criminal associate, is one of the few forms of capital that an arrestee has with law enforcement and prosecutors. There are also paid informants in the barrio's midst. It is common knowledge among the criminal class that without snitches, the police clearance rate (i.e. solved crimes) would be even more dismal than it already is, with no type of crime rising above a 65 percent solved rate nationally (FBI 2015).

Normally, being a reláje carries a stigma, causing one to fall into disrepute in the barrio network. The terminology used to indicate that one is or was a reláje is to say *"tiene cola"* (he has a tail), as in a rat's tail. A generic way to indicate someone's status is to say *"tiene chaqueta"* (he's got a jacket), which is ironic, given this is an old police term to say one is an ex-offender. In the barrio, having a chaqueta or *corrido* usually refers to being a reláje, but it can also mean the person was a child sex offender, a homosexual, or a coward, so it is a generic kind of label. It is also important to point out that there are many false accusations among the criminal class of someone being a reláje. It is common among enemies or competitors in the illegal drug trade. As Fred Carrasco never signed his statement implicating El Chalape to narcotics agents, there is still some doubt about its authenticity among men of that generation, among others.

However stigmatizing in theory, the reality is that *relajándo* is quite a common occurrence in criminal circles. To the extent that primary traits of criminality are selfishness and narcissism (Gottfredson & Hirschi 1990), the snitch's behavior is consistent with what is theorized to be the typical personality profile of the street criminal. When discussing the reputations of known barrio dwellers with my research subjects (a main thrust of this work), if one was ever suspected or known to be a reláje it is usually the first thing said about the person. Although relájes are rather commonplace in the barrio, being a snitch runs contrary to the typical street code (Anderson 1994) and is therefore shunned in these subcultures.

There are several roles or statuses within the criminal subclass that are related to the reláje but that are not directly tied to the street. As touched upon in chapter 3, up until the early 1980s, Texas prisons used the building tender system to maintain order among the inmates. This was a trustee system that relied on certain inmates to police other inmates (Fong 1990). While there were certain advantages to being a building tender, it clearly had its disadvantages in terms of stigma, as is evident in the inmate nickname used to describe the role, *marrano* (pig). Many who assumed this role became the target of violence both in and out of prison. Even if someone was never a reláje on the street, if he became a marrano in prison, the chaqueta typically followed him once back in "the free," earning him some disdain among his fellow barrio dwellers.

A second questionable role related to this general area of stigma in the criminal community, namely among drug addicts, is the former addict turned counselor. This was a common role played by various men upon their return to the community after a prison sentence. The primary residential drug-rehabilitation program where this took place in San Antonio was The Patrician Movement, founded in 1959 by a Catholic priest named Noel Brosnan. It occupied the former St. John's Seminary on an eleven-acre campus in an inner Southeast Side neighborhood, in the turf of the barrio gang La Dot. Over the years, thousands of addicts from throughout the county were treated there, until it finally closed its doors in 2011. The program was known for employing former addicts who had the wherewithal to become peer counselors, and it employed a number of reputable former barrio youth. The most renowned of them was Gilbert "Hippo" Carranza of Taco Village, who is profiled toward the end of chapter 3 as having a number of distinguished accomplishments and other forms of social capital with both the barrio and conventional society. Other well-known members of the barrio who once worked there were Chendo Gonzales (Los Cocos), "Wheaties" (The Circle), Benny Puente

(Calle Guadalupe), Joe Guerrero (Bounds), Raymond "Scorpion" Sorder (Bounds), Eduardo "Walo" Porter (Taco Village), and Willie "Mo" Moreno (Calle Guadalupe). Because part of the role of counselor was to ensure that residents were "clean," the enforcement role was dangerously close to that of the reláje, and it was perceived that way by many whose probation officers found a negative report in their files.

Discussion

Among the most important contexts in forming barrio networks were the bars and taverns in the Bounds and the West Side, primarily. They facilitated much of the action that set the barrio apart, culturally, from other contexts in the city. Analyzing this setting provides a window into the milieu and network properties that produce a figure like Fred Carrasco, a barrio drug kingpin. Where McKinney's (1975) work on Carrasco was the first of its kind in documenting San Antonio Chicano barrio networks of the 1960s and '70s, it barely scratched the surface on this topic. To be fair, McKinney's work was not designed to accomplish this task, but simply to tell the tale of the barrio's most notorious modern villain, or folk hero, depending on the interpretation and viewpoint (Montejano 2010; Olguin 2010).

The Carrasco era marked an important chapter in South Texas's modern drug-smuggling history. Indeed, the violence and related drama that accompanied it on barrio streets and in Texas prisons represent a sea of change in the underworld politics that would govern those settings for the next several decades. The South Texas region is easily one of the most active of the federal government's High Intensity Drug Trafficking Areas Program (HIDTA) designations in the United States. While such narcotics law enforcement operations now have Mexican Drug Trafficking Organizations (DTOs), or cartels, to deal with, in the 1980s and 1990s their efforts were still primarily focused on barrio activities in the major cities. Ties to Mexican suppliers have always been part of the equation in Texas's barrio drug operations (Campbell 2009), but law enforcement targets at this time were mainly prison gang members and their affiliates.

Analyzing the Carrasco era helps us to understand what seem like stark contrasts in the norms and politics of the drug trade in the barrio, going from the old-school norms of the 1940s and 1950s ruedas to that of the extreme and merciless tactics of modern prison gangs. I posit that the Carrasco era, and his organization in particular, provided a model for how the 1980s-generation Texas prison gangs would conduct their business in and out of the prisons. Moreover, since the sentencing of drug offenders became much stiffer in the 1970s (Western 2006), the incarceration binge that followed provided an ample supply of potential recruits for these organizations, so that the fiercest and most capable barrio criminals would run such groups. The next chapter treats these topics with an intergenerational framework, analyzing what is culturally similar or different about Chicano barrio gangsters over the decades, and what role, if any, the older networks, familial, neighborhood, and prison based, may play in modern formations.

Six

The 1980s: Prison Gangs in Ol' San Antone

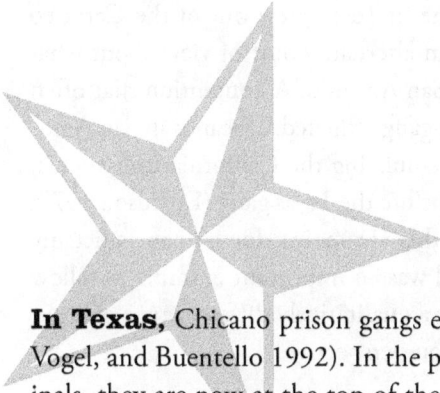

In Texas, Chicano prison gangs emerged in the early 1980s (Fong, Vogel, and Buentello 1992). In the pecking order of barrio street criminals, they are now at the top of the hierarchy. This has been the case in California (Davidson 1974) for much longer than in Texas (Fong 1990; Valdez 2005). This development marks a significant change in the norms that typically govern underworld politics and processes in the state. The Carrasco group pioneered some of the techniques used to terrorize would-be competitors and discipline those within the ranks of the organization in the 1970s, and their brand of violence would become widespread among Chicano prison gangs in Texas throughout the 1980s and '90s. One of the most compelling arguments to support the predecessor theory put forth here and in chapter 5 is the strong geographical connection between Carrasco's group and the most prominent of the Central Texas prison gangs, Mexikanemi (a.k.a. the Texas Mexican Mafia, a.k.a. la Eme).

The home base of the Texas Mexican Mafia is widely known by justice system practitioners and the local public to be San Antonio, just as it was for Fred Carrasco and his clan. Where members of both groups were in barrio gangs in that city as youths, there is a shared background in their general orientation and lived experience, separated by little more than one generation, in most cases. The social conditions of the barrio and experiences of Chicano males with the criminal justice system, for example, are comparable in both eras. Indeed, this study found that some of the children of 1950s and 1960s barrio gang members became prison gang members in one of three major groups operating in San Antonio since the

1980s (la Eme, Texas Syndicate, and Los Pistoleros). For most, the tie is to la Eme, due to its strong presence in that city. Idolized by many young Chicano street gang members of the post-1980s era, la Eme became a household name in the barrios of San Antonio.

Although I contend that la Eme in Texas grew out of the Carrasco group, it is worth noting there is an alternate point of view about what led to the formation of la Eme in San Antonio. A contention that often surfaces among non-Mafia and non-gang affiliated Chicanos in San Antonio is that it is a copycat structure emulating the California Eme model, which originated over twenty years before the Texas gang (Davidson 1974; Valdez & Enriquez 2011). While this viewpoint doesn't contradict my own thesis that the Carrasco model was an important example to follow for the Texas Eme in particular, it is a qualitatively different type of argument that is akin to a gang migration perspective.

Robert Morrill (2007) is a retired correctional officer and gang expert who worked in both California and Texas prison systems. His is the only known, written account of the emulation hypothesis. Although it is essentially a self-published product (by an unrefereed, now defunct local press in San Antonio), it is a plausible statement that documents its sources of information on the topic. Morrill claims that while incarcerated at the California state prison in Lompoc, the future (and current) president of the Texas Mexican Mafia, Heriberto "Herb" Huerta, met with ranking officers of the California *Eme* to gain permission to begin an independent chapter in Texas (San Antonio). However, Morrill's information comes from secondhand accounts, so its reliability is questionable and can only be proven by interviewing Huerta himself, who sits in a maximum security prison in Florence, Colorado.[62]

An intuitive assumption to make about the stark difference in modus operandi of the prison gang generation and that of previous barrio criminal organizations is that it is a product of modernity. That is, the differences in structure and the level of brutality are simply generational or period effects; an evolution or *devolution* of gang violence that escalated in the 1980s nationwide. However, the generational divide between these two San Antonio-based groups in particular was not cleanly demarcated. This study found that a significant number of members of 1950s and 1960s barrio youth gangs were affiliated with a prison gang some twenty-five to thirty years later. This fact calls for a more careful examination of the generational dynamics at play in the world of Chicano gangs over the last several decades.

Old School Vatos and the Chicano Prison Gangs

The standard interview with members of 1950s barrio gangs included questions about the structure, mentality, and overall nature of old-school (pre-1970s) Chicano gangs versus modern ones. The most generic, common response was that "respect has been lost." The senseless victimization of innocent bystanders in episodes of street gang violence, and the intentional targeting or collateral killing of a gang member's family were examples of the decline in values or unwritten rules that once forbade such behaviors.[63] There were also references to the methods of initiation into modern gangs and the paramilitary hierarchy that exists within them as undesirable features.

The criminal careers of many men of the 1950s barrio gang generation tapered off before the emergence of the prison gangs. As do most offenders, either they aged out of their delinquent behavior (Moffitt 2006), or they remained marginally connected to their old barrio networks. For many others whose careers lasted much longer, there was an overlap with the beginning of the prison gang era. For those whose criminal careers lasted well into the 1980s and in some cases beyond, I examine how they related to the prison gang generation. That is, to what extent did they become engaged with these groups? Was there generational friction in the form of competition, or was there peaceful coexistence? Also, what role did familial, neighborhood, and prison-based ties play in these intergenerational relationships? Finally, what is culturally similar or different about Chicano barrio gang norms or the gangsters themselves across these two generations?

There are not many men from the 1950s generation alive today who belong(ed) to prison gangs, but they do exist. They are now in their late seventies, and one senses that, unless they are still incarcerated, they are not very active in the groups' governance or routine business. Involvement in these activities likely peaked for them from about 1985 to 2000. This was an extremely violent era in the history of Texas prison gangs to date. Chicano prison gangs are noted for extorting independent drug dealers and street gangs out of a portion of their profits with the threat of violent consequences for resistance (Valdez 2005). Other sources of violence are the "blood in" initiations (attacks on rivals), the killing of its own members for transgressions against the group, small wars with prison gangs of other races, and bloody wars between rival Chicano gangs on the street and in prison (*San Antonio Express-News* 1989).

Given these features of the prison gangs' "business," the first question to address becomes how big a break from the norms of prior generations do current gang practices represent? For the members of 1950s generation gangs who became involved with these later groups, perhaps not much difference exists in their orientation toward the costs and methods of doing business. The murdering of a rival or a snitch was certainly part of the subculture of the ruedas of the 1940s and '50s, but the main difference is that incidents were sporadic and aimed at particular individuals. By comparison, such activities in the modern era of prison gangs became highly systematic. These might be period effects, i.e., an evolution or sign of the times, since the United States as a whole experienced a surge of gang activity and homicides beginning in the 1980s (Bjerregaard and Lizotte 1995; Howell 1999). Or in this case, perhaps prison gangs are a selection mechanism for the most calculating, ruthless individuals within the Chicano criminal subclass. There is evidence of this in the recruitment structure of these groups from street gangs and prison inmates (Tapia; 2013; Tapia et al. 2014), covered later in this chapter.

To evidence the similarities in the boldness of criminal methods used by both 1950s and prison-gang generations, the latter are renowned for "collecting the dime" (Valdez 2005). This is a street tax on non-mafia drug dealers. It is enforced, initially, with a verbal threat, a *calentada* (roughing-up), or if it occurs with a visit to the dealer's home, may include the taking of the cash, drugs, and weapons on site. Forced entry and armed robbery at a person's home or dwelling is now commonly referred to as a "home invasion" through routine media coverage of such incidents. In traditional barrio street jargon (Appendix C), this is known as *hikiando,* or as *getting jacked* in contemporaneous gangsta subculture. In the barrio, this practice goes back at least to the 1950s, as told by this study's interviewees. Here, again, the difference is that it was a sporadic, opportunistic, and individually driven event in previous eras rather than a systematic practice with prison gangs' dealings on the street.

Mutual Respect and Intergenerational Friction

I explored the topic of relationships between the 1950s barrio gangster generation and the prison gang generation with my research subjects. Most men of the 1950s barrios, whether early criminal "desisters" or those with lengthier careers, expressed resentment for the prison gangs' manner of conducting business. Most men of this generation managed to avoid any formal involvement with prison gangs. This stance was common even among those who were incarcerated during the groups' formation in Texas prisons. Part of this is due to the tribalism that occurs in the Texas prison system, where geographic nativism is an important basic organizer. As the primary level of group affiliation and allegiance, those "old-school" gangsters of the 1950s and '60s are typically afforded respect by San Antonio's younger generation of offenders—and by those from other places, as well.[64]

A 1950s barrio gangster who spent about two-fifths of his adult life in prison stated, "I was asked by [prison gang] if I wanted to join, but I said 'no, I want to be able to get out [of prison] and go home' (laughs)" (Interviewee #2). Another interviewee (#4) with a similar profile, except that he had been a GI, made a similar statement about himself and his brother, who both did time in state and federal systems: "*En un tiempo, [prison gang] nos ofrecieron a mi y a mi hermano posiciones altos con ellos, pero al fin les decimos que chale.*" (At one time [prison gang] offered ranking positions to my brother and me, but in the end, we decided against it.)

On Competition and Coexistence

Given prison gangs' self-described purpose and routine practice of charging "the dime" to independent or street-gang affiliated drug dealers and engaging in other forms of extortion, it was important that the study explore their relationship to old-timers who were still in business themselves. On this topic, subject comments were overwhelmingly suggestive of a peaceful coexistence between the generations. To offer some perspective, the 1950s barrio gang generation was generally in their mid-forties when prison gangs emerged in San Antonio. In those days (mid-1980s), the prison gang members and the 1950s gangsters were separated by little more than half a generation, or ten to twenty years, in most cases. Since it is not likely that seasoned, veteran criminals would be willing to pay the dime or succumb to other forms of intimidation by younger groups, this may have set the tone for the next twenty years or so. One subject commented that prison gangs "basically left these guys alone *porque no los podian gorriliar*" (because they couldn't bully them). They might say to themselves, "Hey these old guys are crazy, man" (#6). Moreover, the leaders of these groups knew a lot of the older guys via family and other network ties and mostly instructed their soldiers to lay off of them unless they were affiliated with a rival prison gang.

Other key dimensions to the generational dynamic involve the family networking components. Recall from chapter 3 that only about nine of eighty-one children (10 percent) of the 1950s generation sample were prison gang members. This is the number that was verifiable or that was admitted to, but I suspect it was much higher. The reasons for possible concealment of this fact by subjects are several. First, there is the potential stigma associated with this for all of the reasons discussed so far in this chapter regarding generational differences in gang philosophy. Second, there is the secrecy that comes with prison gang subculture, which is well understood and upheld by family members. Finally, there is the cultural norm to avoid discussing with outsiders the status, fate, or lot of family members, especially that of grown children. The barrio's harsh socioeconomic conditions and lack of opportunity structures creates many negative outcomes associated with the modern underclass framework that are not always pleasant to discuss with outsiders.

To the extent that the children and other younger family members of 1950s gang members became involved with prison gangs, the fluidity of intergenerational ties between what at first appear to be distinct groups becomes clearer. Such ties are perhaps how some members of the 1950s barrio generation became formally involved with prison gangs. Moreover, although the rules of recruitment, initiation, expectations for comportment, and rank structure are clearly spelled out for each gang, there are likely to be elder advisers who may or may not be formally part of the group. Furthermore, these groups have now existed for long enough that younger generations are now in ranking positions, and many of the older shot-callers have gone into "retirement." Yet, because these groups employ a strict paramilitary rank structure, some of the original figureheads, now in their seventies, still hold titles such as president, vice president, and general. While many details of the structure of Latino prison gangs have become public knowledge through news media and television documentary coverage of the topic, these practical nuances regarding its deeper network structure have not.

The role of the prison experience in defining the intergenerational network structure of adult Chicano gangs is just as profound as that of familial ties. Often, the two are intertwined. Where much of the history of Texas prison gangs involves, at times, bloody rivalries, constant tension, and splintering among the various factions, there are subnetwork features to explore. Discharge from prison, whether through parole or completion of the sentence, is also key in this arena. As a symbiotic relationship between prison gangs and "the streets" exists (Morrill 2007; Valdez et al. 2009; Valdez and Enriquez 2011), some of these relationships are decades old. Men who were enemies in the barrio gang days of the 1950s and '60s often found themselves in rival prison gangs as adults, and targeted each other in the 1980s as a result. Some of these rivalries also exemplify intergenerational conflict and violence, because if a ranking member of one group puts a "green light" on a member of another group, he can send younger soldiers to (attempt to) do the job. One interviewee (#13) described how one of these cases involved a well-known "old-school" barrio member from the 1950s who was a prison gang member in middle age. There were constant attempts on his life out in "the free" by the rival prison gang, which he survived because of his aggressive defensive posture. Valdez (2005) illustrated how this scenario repeated itself in wars between street and prison gangs of the subsequent cohort in the 1990s.

In his now-classic analysis of Chicano outlaws, bandits, gang members, etc., Alfredo Mirandé (1987) wrote that the hierarchy from street to prison gang was an understudied, poorly understood topic. He went on to describe the decades-old East Los Angeles barrio gang, Hoyo MaraVilla, as a feeder group to la Eme in California. The same phenomenon is present in San Antonio, evidencing the role of barrio street gangs in defining the broader, multigenerational network. Although he used thinly disguised pseudonyms to code the actual gang names, Avelardo Valdez (2005) discussed these types of connections in San Antonio. It appears from his work, and from my own fieldwork on this issue, that one of the longest-standing barrio gangs in San Antonio, Varrio La Blanca from the San Juan Courts, became a feeder group to Los Pistoleros prison gang at some point in the 1990s. This alliance came about because leaders of VLB had been extorted for profits by another prison gang who were rivals of the Pistoleros. These rivals, in turn, recruited the leaders of several large Chicano street gangs in other West Side public housing projects to help them enforce their ten percent decree (more details in chapter 7).

The Caliber Spectrum of Chicano Gang Members

Those involved in ghetto and barrio gangs vary on a host of items relative to their identities as hustlers and gangsters. They vary in their levels of delinquent and criminal propensity, sophistication, and dedication to "the life," i.e., their street embeddedness (Bernburg, Krohn, & Rivera, 2006; Pyrooz, Sweeten, & Piqero 2013). Those that exhibit high levels in all these areas, and who develop reputations as capable drug dealers or violent enforcers as youth, may be good candidates to enter prison gangs. For those with family members who are involved in these groups, their odds of joining are especially high (Valdez 2005). Fong et al. (1992) listed the average age of the various Latino Texas prison gangs as about thirty-one years old, which reflects a more seasoned offender, perhaps approaching the prime of their criminal career.

The generational dynamics covered in this chapter revealed that Texas prison gang involvement has quite a broad age spectrum. The average age Fong et al. (1992) reported strictly reflects institutional data, and was calculated at an early stage in the development of these groups, before many of the inmates paroled and expanded their operations to the streets. The average age of members of these same prison gangs in 2015, drawn from the San Antonio Police Department gang database, yields a broader age structure with a higher average age—late thirties (Glass 2015). This is because it now reflects the ages of non-incarcerated members and shows the maturation of these groups since their inception. Yet, as noted earlier, there is much "new blood" in these organizations, as recruitment of promising prospects is an ongoing feature of the groups.

In terms of the criminogenic potential, or proven street savvy of prison gang prospects, Latino prison gangs are likely composed of the barrio's most elite gangsters. Although it is slightly less so today, recruitment has traditionally been well structured and very restrictive. There are various stages of acceptance into a Latino prison gang in Texas, beginning with serving as *esquina* (backup) for conflicts with other groups.

A more distinguished level of recognition by the prison gang that could ultimately result in becoming a prospect[ive] member is *esquina firme*. Sponsorship by a full-fledged member is required for one to be selected as a *prospecto*, and a probationary period is required, typically within which the prospect will carry out some important aspect of business for the group. In most organizations, a majority vote is needed for a prospect to be *confirmado* as a member. Interestingly, the language used to classify an inmate as a member of a security threat group (gang) by the Texas prison system is to "confirm" him.

The potential recruit into a Texas Latino prison gang typically comes from a street-oriented family (see chapters 3 and 7), and is known to law enforcement by virtue of his lengthy or violent criminal history, often extending to his juvenile street gang days. These individuals were not marginal members of youth gangs, but usually held leadership positions or were loyal soldiers with lucrative skills in auto theft, burglary, armed robbery, and the like. A willingness and reputation for meting out violence against rivals also makes one a valuable asset to a street gang, even if it is the individual's main or sole contribution. A potential prison gang recruit thus possesses a high street IQ, but this is not always sufficient for full recruitment or survival within the group if recruited. If such an individual aspires to become a prison gang member, whether he will advance to recruitment and survival within the group also depends on his actual IQ, levels of self-control, and charisma. Prison gangs tend to be highly regimented organizations whose members must exercise self-discipline to stay within the constitutional and informal rules of the group. This includes sharing profits, obtaining permission from superiors for certain actions, and following orders, some of which are extreme actions such as committing homicide. The inability of many members to follow these rules, coupled with intra-group politics and power struggles, has resulted in dozens of intra-group murders and dozens of absconds (members who leave the gang)[65] over the years.

Texas Latino Gangs in Theoretical Perspective

Given the high levels of internal strife that have plagued the Texas Latino prison gangs in their brief history to date, evaluating the stock of individuals eligible for recruitment provides interesting fodder for criminological theorizing. On several occasions during my field research, my elderly research subjects posed the question of "whether [a certain prison gang] still exists." In light of the extent to which these older men's street networks are intertwined with modern ones, this is an important and telling question. In 2009 and 2010, several gang officers from various agencies who were guest lecturers at my criminal justice courses at UT-San Antonio also commented to me (in private) that they felt the era of prison gangs was in decline.[66]

Chapter 3 examined the varying levels of human capital found among a sample of 1950s barrio gang members and concluded that aside from a few constants like poverty, predicting membership presented something of a black box. How then, should we consider prison gang members in this regard? I have argued that they represent an elite class of street criminals. If so, why have the organizations they built evidenced such high levels of dysfunction; or is this even a fair assessment? That is, should outlaw organizations competing for control of underworld markets, power, and prestige be evaluated any differently on structural integrity or capacity from the way we evaluate legitimate entities in the open marketplace, or partisan political groups prone to splintering?

Should the criminal organizations of elite members of the Chicano outlaw class be judged by a different standard *because* they emerge from the underclass, where the norms that govern are largely outside the mainstream? For example, in terms of organizational analysis, what should we make of prison gangs' use of street justice to regulate their "marketplace" in the absence of a legal regulatory body?[67] In terms of potential or capacity for organizational survival, we don't berate the short-lived La Raza Unida political party in Texas or MoveOn.org for being mere blips in the broader spectrum of party politics, or suspect their educated leaders of being incompetent. Then it is perhaps not fair to consider the leaders or members of Texas prison gangs or other large, street-level criminal groups as incapable of managing higher-order organizational operations simply because they are from the streets and lack formal education, or because as proven criminals, they are thought to be overtly self-interested. In sociological terms, one commits the "ecological fallacy" by attributing to individuals the characteristics of their larger groupings, subcultures, or organizations operating in the broader societal context (Freedman 2002). Yet, we do, in practical analyses, often commit the fallacy with generalized beliefs or statements about *the types of people* drawn to these groups, or in criminological terms, those with the *propensity* to join such groups.

For more perspective on this question of the value of recruits or of the eligible pool of recruits into prison gang organizations over time, the final portion of this chapter discusses the hierarchy that exists from the street to the prison gang. I focus on the hybrid groups that have occupied a nebulous place in the hierarchy in all regions of Texas where prison gangs exist. While these groups have recently organized to challenge the prison gangs' authority in lockup facilities and on the streets, there is an interesting recent history to tell, now spanning several decades. Doing so provides valuable insights on widespread individual aspirations to be part of the reputable and feared Chicano prison gangs, and how the gangs used this to their organizational advantage for several decades.

Tangos: **Texas's Street-Prison Hybrids**

As described earlier in this chapter, the most basic organizational principle for the gang population in Texas jails and prisons is geography, or more specifically, the inmates' jurisdiction (hometown). This is especially true of gang-involved Latino inmates, where subgroupings occur by major Texas cities and regions. Over time, these largely metro-based subgroupings developed rivalries and alliances with other factions, both within and between cities. Now, perhaps equally as salient as these city-based identifiers, are the intergenerational dynamics at work. A recent but common observation of those concerned with prison gang developments in Texas is that intergenerational conflict has been underway for the past decade among Latino gangs, an issue that possibly dates back to the late 1990s. Prison-site documentaries and other media depictions of this phenomenon also exist (Eiserer, 2008; History Channel, 2008; National Geographic, 2010), reinforcing and perhaps fueling this tension.

Where the strains that intergenerational conflict has placed on Texas jails and prisons appear to be significant (Tapia 2013; Tapia et al. 2014), such conflict has yet to be met with adequate research or policy attention. So far, only cursory descriptions of the newly emerged prison factions and a smattering of police intelligence efforts on their "free world" activities have surfaced (Texas Department of Public, 2011; 2015). I examine the state's recent history of street-to-prison hybrid formations and the intergenerational conflicts that ensued for added perspective on the question of the caliber of gang members and the hierarchical structure of Chicano gangs. I focus the discussion on San Antonio's dynamics specifically, to continue to document significant benchmarks in that city's timeline of the Chicano gang phenomenon.

Tango History and Its Break from Gang Hierarchy

For the last several decades, many young Latino inmates in Texas prisons, especially those with prior street-gang affiliations, have gravitated to city-based sub-groups known as Tangos. These groups have traditionally been affiliated with Latino prison gangs, which function as parent organizations. A young Latino inmate from a given Texas city who was imprisoned might choose to "roll with" or "represent" his hometown while serving out his sentence (Texas Department of Public Safety, 2007). This was done for protection, camaraderie, and/or as a natural extension of his street-gang affiliation. The deeper implication was that the inmate served as part of a reserve army for the prison gang and might be asked to perform illegal acts within the facility to benefit that parent group.

Historically, then, Tangos were not only considered foot soldiers, but the fiercely loyal among them achieved a more distinguished level of recognition that could ultimately result in becoming a recruit of the prison gang. Each higher level of affiliation carried both increased privileges and respect among Latino prison gangs and other inmates generally. It appears, however, that playing the role of foot soldier was not historically a rewarding experience for most Tangos. By many informal accounts, too few of them were afforded the opportunity to become full-fledged recruits despite putting in ample "work" in the penitentiary to become worthy of consideration for membership.[68] In short, the reward structure of the parent group failed to accommodate a large base of gang hopefuls over time. The widely heard claim among gang and non-gang members alike is that too many young Chicanos were being used and filtered out by the existing hierarchical system, leading to the disillusionment of the next generation of would-be recruits (Eiserer, 2008; History Channel, 2008; National Geographic, 2010).

Changing Mantras, Changing Structures

Whether to avoid the stigma of classification as a Security Threat Group in prison or for ideological or other functional reasons, the Tangos of the current generation have so far resisted the prison gang label. Members of these loosely affiliated groups claim they are a support network for inmates who want to do their time peacefully and avoid coercion from traditional Latino prison gangs. According to recently filmed documentaries and other media accounts, the acronym TANGO has been reclaimed and re-identified by the younger generation of Latino inmates to mean "Together Against Negative Gang Organizations" (Eiserer, 2008). Similarly, according to several Tango members and members of its parent group,[69] Orejon, the San Antonio-based Tango has also taken on a different meaning from that of the past few decades. By these accounts, OREJON is newly construed as an acronym meaning "One Race Equally Joined Or Nothing," a far cry from its prior connotation: that it was the eyes and *ears* (i.e. *oreja*) of the Texas Mexican Mafia.

These mantras reflect a changing mind-set among the new generation toward a horizontal versus a hierarchical structure, and a new function for the Tango-type organization in Texas jails and prisons. Some of the most relevant theoretical and policy questions include whether a transition from the defensive posturing of Tangos to one in which they assume the organizational characteristics of the traditional gangs is inevitable.[70] Recent *Texas Gang Threat Assessments* now rank various Tango factions very high on law enforcement priority lists (Texas Department of Public Safety 2011; 2015). Theoretical work on prison gang formation within the California state system offers some of the potential structural if not cultural dynamics driving this phenomenon.

Assuming that gangs in the correctional setting form for protection, as is the claim made by the Tangos, Skarbeck (2012) discussed how a capable defense illustrates the power and ability to go on the offense. Inmates establish order among themselves on a level below that of official facility governance, giving rise to the inmate code and the development of convict norms. Issues such as overcrowding, scarce resources, and cultural or racial differences create the need for subgovernance. However, when a larger proportion of inmates have never previously served time, the norms associated with the inmate code are less effective where "new inmates misinterpret and disregard signaling mechanisms and disrupt the social system more frequently" (Skarbeck, 2012: 23).

When new inmates are unfamiliar with the convict code, they are reprimanded or perhaps bullied by inmate leaders, who, in effect, are also the prison gang leaders (Davidson 1974; Jacobs 1974). The newer class of inmates eventually reaches some tipping point in terms of size or shared negative experiences, then seeks an alternate method of providing governance; hence, a new organization is born in the facility. Using prison data for California, Skarbeck (2012) illustrated that the rise of prison gangs in the 1950s and 1960s corresponded to a dramatic rise in the size of the prison population and a much younger age structure. This suggests that demographic changes made norms less effective and led to more inmate conflict, a thesis that is explored for Texas's Tango subclass elsewhere (see Tapia et al. 2014).

In the context of this discussion, the elements affecting the collective conscience of the Tangos have implications for theory regarding the organizational capacity of Chicano gang members. To note that the Tangos, a historically subservient group to the prison gangs, have, in such a short timeframe, evolved a collective mind-set of rebellion, rejection of traditional gang norms, reformation, and resistance is additional evidence of the rationality of the Chicano gang population. If, in fact, the Tango groupings, whose individual members supposedly lacked the wherewithal (in gang terms, the *cora* [heart], *esnape* [smarts], etc.) to become part of the elite group, are capable of this large-scale (statewide) reorganizing, it is noteworthy. It may even speak to the political consciousness of Chicano gang factions, which in this case somewhat resembles a form of Marxism. Given the high mortality rate among members of the elite groups, often murdered by their own organizations, Tango developments seem to represent an evolved form of rationality that resists the power-hungry model for which the ultimate goal is gang prestige.

Summary and Discussion

The timeline in this chapter cuts across several decades to address generational friction among the adult Chicano gang population resulting from changing norms and politics in the barrio. It depicts how the Latino prison gangs of the 1980s and 1990s related to the older (pre-1960s) and younger generations (Tangos) over time. It began with the thesis that the structure and violent nature of the most notable San Antonio-based prison gang (la Eme) was heavily influenced by the Fred Carrasco cross-national drug gang of the early 1970s. Aside from the specific barrio and prison roots he shared with the leaders of la Eme, he had a particular style of governance that was reflected in the orientation of prison gangs. As Carrasco required his close operatives to take sworn oaths of allegiance to the group, so have mafia norms been structured. The level of brutality utilized by Carrasco to intimidate and co-opt competitors and to maintain discipline among his employees are also features of the Latino prison gangs that emerged in the 1980s in San Antonio and the region.

Texas prison gangs emerged in an age of technological advance on all fronts, and the advanced tools of their trade enabled them to threaten and perpetrate violence in unprecedented proportions. This level of brutality was a clear break from the barrio gang norms of the past, creating a notorious reputation for the Latino prison gang genre that many of the 1950s barrio gang generation resented. A source of constant debate among the broad spectrum of persons interviewed for this study is the level of courage and ferocity of the typical Chicano street gang member over time (i.e. which generation was the "toughest"). As the weapons and methods used in violent confrontations of the 1950s generation called for much more close-up and personal tactics, naturally the contention of this generation is they had more honor and "guts" than contemporary Chicano gang members. Chapter 3 also showed there are serious misconceptions about the intensity of the 1950s gang subculture and associated violence. Nevertheless, these interviewees were always careful to provide the prison gangs their due respect, clearly because the gangs are considered to be volatile, reckless, and vindictive.

Interestingly, a younger generation of Chicano prison gang hopefuls developed a fierce resistance to the prison gangs after several decades of being a critical part of their hierarchy. Like the 1950s and '60s generations of gangsters, they developed a collective disdain for the prison gangs' norms and methods of governance. It appears that in the long term, community norms, particular in this case to the Chicano working class and underclass, a gang model utilizing such levels of brutality and elitism may not be sustainable. Prominent research on this topic shows that US Latinos and Mexican American populations in particular are far less violent than their black counterparts for example (Martinez 2014; Sampson et al. 2005). There is thus widespread fear and resentment of prison gangs in the Chicano community. As violent as barrio gangs are reputed to be, the 1950s and '60s groups "stood for something," since they were rooted in local neighborhood turfs and tradition. Compared to those groups and to the non-gang population, the extreme levels of violence among prison gangs may be seen as pathological, as they violate long-held community value systems of respect for the barrio (Duran 2012; Moore and Pinderhughes 1993). That is, such violence may be seen as unnatural in the order of barrio processes because it is uncharacteristic of "true" neighborhood norms to extort legitimate businesses. Even the extortion of street gangs and other criminal groups that profit in the underground marketplace is frowned upon by many.

As an important qualifier to end this chapter, just as the generational divide between 1950s gangsters and the prison-gang era gangsters was far from universal, such is the case with the younger generation of prison-gang hopefuls. There is no standard age or status cutoff for demarcating between members of Tangos and prison gangs, for example. Rather, this can be quite a fluid continuum. Although faction-based dynamics are fueled by a younger cohort's frustration with the status quo of the old guard, one of the nuances here is that many younger inmates, for familial reasons and out of preference for the lore or prestige that for so long has attached to the traditional Latino prison gangs, continue to be recruited into these groups. Therefore, age is not an absolute determinant of Tango membership. The next chapter thus takes the discussion back to San Antonio's barrio street scene (1980s to 2015) to continue to evaluate the changes in norms and trends in that city's Chicano youth gang population over time.

Seven
Modern Chicano Street Gangs: 1990s to 2015

The modern Chicano street gang is examined in this penulti-mate chapter, giving consideration to both the permanency and changes among barrio gangs over time. I will investigate whether the etiology and other features of the modern Chicano barrio gang resemble the archetypes found here and in past work on these groups. The chapter will further explore how modern groups compare to their predecessors' street-corner orientation, where boyhood play groups evolved into more insidious ones. Furthermore, what is the role of modernity, mass media, and technology in altering the size of the gang population and influenc-ing its subcultural characteristics, gang recruitment processes, and the network structure depicted throughout the book? Might one still expect to find substantial network links across the generations, for example?

To address these questions, I continue to detail the San Antonio Chicano gang evolutionary timeline established in previous chapters, picking it up here in the late 1980s. The youth gang phenomenon proliferated tremendously in the 1980s and 1990s in San Antonio and across the United States. (Casil-las 1994; Klein 1995; Spergel et al. 2005; Sykes 1997). This surge was espe-cially profound in San Antonio, where it was likened to a fad but with violent and often deadly consequences. An article in the *Texas Monthly* covered San Antonio Chicano youth gangs and found that many otherwise mainstream youth became swept up in the epidemic. That is, in addition to participation by genuine ghetto and barrio youth, many middle and high school athletes and "good" students developed a brief but intense interest in guns and gang warfare (Duff 1994). Gini Sykes (1997) also documented this widespread fas-cination with the gang life in wealthier areas of San Antonio, earning the city the dubious distinction of being the "drive-by capital" of the United States.[71]

Modern Gang-Crime Indicators in San Antonio

Gang crime data are notoriously unreliably coded, and estimates vary depending on whether counts of gang-related incidents are restricted to those that are clearly gang-motivated (e.g. drive-by shootings) or extended to count those that simply involve documented gang members (e.g. domestic violence, theft) (Greene and Pranis 2007; Klein 1995; 2004; Maxson and Klein 2001). The reporting of gang crimes is not a requirement of the FBI in its collection of official data from agencies; therefore many police departments do not make this distinction public, if they collect the data at all. Where records do exist, unless a researcher builds rapport with police officials or data gatekeepers, this is often among the most difficult crime data to obtain. This is true of San Antonio, where the police culture can be characterized as somewhat secretive. Some have noted that the categorization of crime incidents as gang-related can be a political process (Huff 1989), especially for tourism-oriented cities like San Antonio (Sikes 1997).

Youth violence in the United States peaked in 1993 (FBI, 2002; Snyder 2003), as did gang violence in particular (Howell 1999). In terms of gang versus non-gang, one type of violent crime where the motive is usually more reliably coded than it is with other crimes is homicide. A reduction in gang violence was evident in San Antonio, as shown in Figure 1,

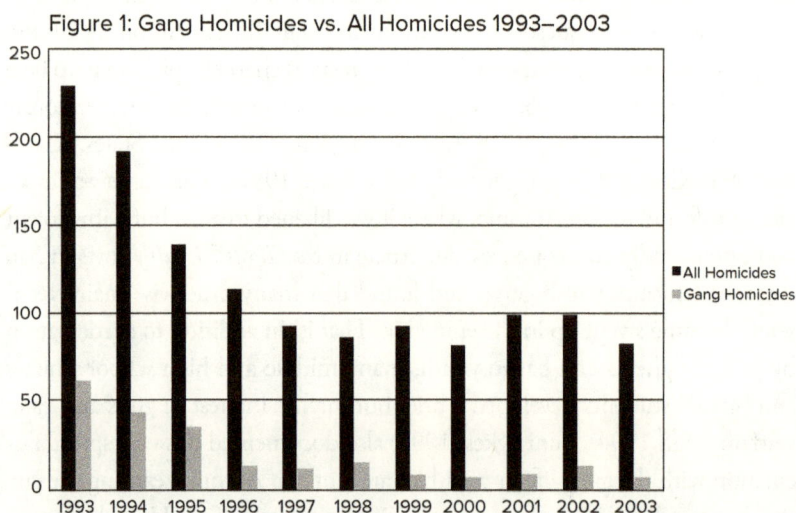

Figure 1: Gang Homicides vs. All Homicides 1993–2003

which shows the proportion of homicides that were gang related for an eleven-year period (SAPD 2004). Gang-related homicide was highest in 1993, mirroring the national trend. About 15.7 percent of San Antonio homicides were gang related throughout this decade, which is a comparable estimate to the national rate (Greene and Pranis 2007).

Another crime that is nearly invariably gang-related is drive-by shooting. Figure 2 contains counts of these events in San Antonio for 1993-2003. Whereas there is some fluctuation over time, as in the case of homicides, the number of drive-by incidents seemed to have stabilized at a much lower level after a significant drop in incidents in 1994 and again in 1997. The peak of 1,262 in 1993, when the county's population size was about one million, produced a drive-by rate of 126.2 per 100,000 in that year. It is an alarming rate, but it is not known how it compares to that of Chicago or Los Angeles, which were hotbeds of gang activity in the early 1990s as well.

Violent episodes in general (fatal and non-fatal) are a much less reliable measure of gang-related crime than homicides or drive-by shootings. This is for a complex set of reasons, such as the investigating officer's skill and discretion, the lack of third-party witnesses, witness fear of retaliation, and the subcultural street-code norm that prohibits snitching

Figure 2: Total Drive-by Shootings 1993–2003

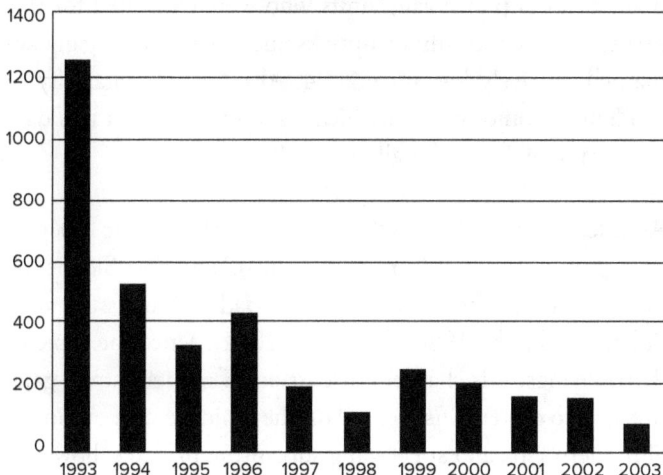

Figure 3: Violent crimes committed by Gang members

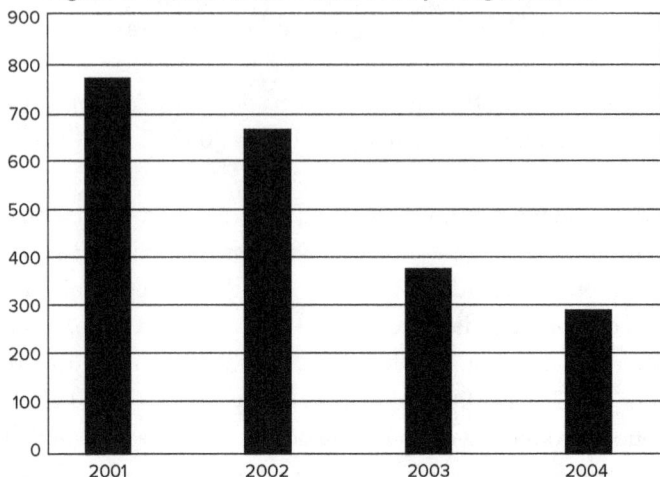

or *relajando* by cooperating with authorities, among other numerous factors. Nonetheless, the data for San Antonio, presented in Figure 3, is available for a restricted number of years. The number of gang-related violent incidents[72] drastically decreased between 2001 and 2004.

Overall, the data in Figures 1 through 3 show a declining volume of gang-related violent incidents in San Antonio over time, with marked decreases from 1993 levels, and a stabilization in the most recent years. Various members of local police gang units who were consulted for this project revealed that even with minor upticks and fluctuations, gang activity has remained relatively low since 2004. Although the majority of gang activity in San Antonio involves Chicanos, a limitation of this data is that it includes gang incidents for all races.

African Americans have historically comprised about 8 to 10 percent of the city's population (US Census 2015 (a)). The East Side is the traditionally black community area, and it has had serious issues with street gang violence since the 1980s (Martinez 2014). Since the topic of this study is barrio gangs, this chapter's discussion of modern street-gang activity, culture, and so on remains focused on the Chicano case. An interesting facet of modern Chicano street-gang subculture in Texas, however, is that many Chicano youth gangs are now culturally ghettoized. That is, many of them mimic the values, norms, speech, and other cultural identifiers of black gangsters—a topic that will be taken up later in this chapter.

The Scope of the Gang Problem, Revisited

One of the more interesting exercises for me in studying San Antonio gangs is to periodically examine a list of all gang names in the San Antonio Police Department's gang database. I often did this as an in-class exercise with my students at UT-San Antonio to consider the potential frivolity of the "gang problem" and how error prone the process of documentation is. In 2015, the gang list contained about three hundred delinquent and criminal groups of all sorts to include tagging (graffiti) crews, party crews, street gangs, prison gangs, and motorcycle gangs. In various years prior, these groups numbered well over one thousand. At first glance, one could easily get the impression that San Antonio continues to be overrun with gang activity as it appears to have been in the early 1990s. Yet the appearance of a large number of group names in the database over the years is as much a product of police protocol for identifying gangs and of other organizational aspects of the police department as it is a result of the actual size of the delinquent and criminal subculture in the city.

The modern definition of a gang used by law enforcement agencies throughout the country is some variant of the following: "three or more persons who identify by a name, color, or symbol, and who organize for delinquent or criminal activity" (Barrows and Huff 2009: 684; NGIC 2016: 4). How to define gangs is a century-old debate in the United States (Ball and Decker 1995), and while the law enforcement definition is functional for statutory and prosecutorial purposes, it has oversimplified the matter for documentation purposes on the street, leading to a broadened definition of the "gang problem." In any given period, the intensity and longevity of most of the groups in the San Antonio police gang database are not impressive, which is the case with most police databases in large cities (Kennedy 2009). Many groups can be characterized as "wannabe" or relatively benign groups that embrace the style and minor forms of delinquency—a reflection of the widespread glorification of "gangsta" subculture in rap music and other media (Kubrin 2005).

The literature on the counting of gangs and gang members clearly shows that it is an inexact process, at best (Ball and Decker 1995; Curry and Decker 1997; Esbensen et al. 2001; Jacobs 2009; Kennedy 2009). Recall the discussion in chapter 4 of this book noting the wildly divergent estimates of San Antonio's youth gang prevalence reported by the press, the police, and intervention specialists in the 1950s. This illustrates that the scope of "the gang problem" has been a poorly understood and politicized issue for decades. These groups are secretive and dynamic, so that a precise identification of them, their structures, and their activities is elusive at best—and therefore prevalence estimates are prone to vary widely. It does not appear that our observations have gotten much more accurate in recent decades, either.

Within three years of its formation in 1991, the SAPD Gang Unit had identified three hundred gangs citywide, one hundred of which were considered serious (Duff 1994). Then, in a 1995 survey, the agency reported San Antonio had 797 gangs, more than double the number reported just a few years prior (Tripplett 1997). Curiously, the data in Figures 1-3 showed that violent gang crime was on a marked decline during these years. In 2006, there were 887 gangs in the SAPD database, and by 2007 the number had jumped to 1,443 (SAPD 2007). By contrast, in his extensive data collection effort on hardcore Chicano gang members in San Antonio throughout the mid and late 1990s, Avelardo Valdez (2005) reported that there were twenty-six serious turf gangs in the Chicano-dominant sectors of the city (West and South Sides). Thus, the script had flipped from the 1950s and 1960s scenario, back when gang researchers discovered far more gangs than city government agencies were willing to admit existed. Sykes (1997) wrote that this change occurred sometime in the late 1980s, when federal grant funds to combat gang activity became available, prompting San Antonio to finally admit to its gang problem.

The Serious Modern Gangs in San Antonio

There is a sizeable group of street gangs in San Antonio, both Chicano and black, that were formed during the vast proliferation of the 1980s and 1990s and that lasted two or three decades, with some of them still around today. These are the well-organized groups that police and 1990s-era San Antonio gang researchers have paid the most attention to for their delinquent, criminal, and violent tendencies. In informational presentations to various groups in 2012, veteran gang unit officers of the SAPD stated that they monitored seventy serious gangs in the city. In that same year, members of the county's juvenile probation gang unit stated there were about 235 groups they considered to be active and worth monitoring. As the latter agency deals with juveniles exclusively, they are better positioned to know about new groups capable of violence. In line with Valdez's (2005) earlier count, the Edgewood Independent School District, located in the heart of the high-poverty Chicano West Side, documented about forty street gangs in the 2012-2013 school year.

In 1997, a report on youth gangs was released by the Texas Law Enforcement Management and Administrative Statistics Program, a component of a federal Bureau of Justice Statistics (BJS). In this report, the five most serious gangs in San Antonio identified by the local gang unit were the Ambrose, the LA Boyz, Bad Company (the BCs), the West Side Varrio (WSV) Kings, and the Wheatley Courts Gangsters (the WCGs). The latter group was the only black gang on the list and it emerged out of the largest housing project in the predominantly black East Side. The WSV Kings were said to be the largest group in the city, with about one thousand members (Tripplett 1997). The Kings and the Ambrose, are, in theory, sets of larger gang "nations" imported from Chicago (this topic is discussed further below). The remaining three, however are homegrown gangs. The BCs and the LA Boyz had deep, multigenerational roots in San Antonio's West Side, and had undergone a name change from previous generations. As described in chapter 3, the BCs appear to have derived from the notorious Ghost Town gang of the 1950s. Similarly, the LA Boyz appear to be descendants of a group called El Con in the 1950s. The contemporary groups occupied the same turf as the 1950s gangs, and in the case of the LA Boyz, the multigenerational link was also based on Lanier High, the quintessential barrio school in the heart of the poverty-stricken West Side. Given what is known about the stability of Chicano residential patterns, especially in high-poverty communities where gangs thrive (Moore et al. 1983), coupled with the current study's finding that gang families tend not to relocate for decades in many cases, it is likely that many modern gang members were the blood relatives of members of the past generations of those neighborhood gangs. Regarding the delinquent and criminal intensity of these groups, several core members of El Con became prison gang members and were known for having murdered other well-known gang members. As described by Valdez (2005), leaders of the LA Boyz (referred to as the "Chicano Dudes" in his published studies) also graduated to prison gang member status.

To the extent that the police account is a reliable measure of the top youth gangs in the city, these rankings are certainly valid. After all, police are the ones who investigate gang violence and their various non-violent activities. That other gang-savvy individuals, including surviving members of the 1990s generation of youth gangs, will agree with the top five ranking is far from guaranteed, however. The prevalence and intensity of the Chicano street gang phenomenon in San Antonio in that era, while likely overstated by police, was still very high. This means there were a large number of groups at war, constantly trying to one-up one another in revenge-based violence and in other forms of reputation-forming gang activity. The next sections will inventory the hard-core Chicano street gangs in San Antonio and will address some of the well-known rivalries, starting with the enemies of several of the four so-called "most serious" Chicano groups. As done with the 1950s gangs in earlier chapters, details of their origins and structure (where known) are offered.

Damage, Inc., who like other groups developed ties to prison gangs in the 1990s, was an extremely violent foe of the LA Boyz. They were a West Side gang from the Guadalupe and Nineteenth Street area west of the Cassiano Courts. Interestingly, the name of this group exemplifies the intermingling of youth subcultures during this era. To youth of the 1980s and 1990s, "Damage Incorporated" is a clear reference to a popular and aggressive heavy metal song of the band Metallica. Other serious rivals of the LA Boyz included the 2-6, the WSV Kings, and the WSV Kings' younger cohort, the Big Time Kings (BTKs). The BTKs were a very large gang who, despite their implied affiliation to the (Latin) Kings' nation, started out as a dance group in the Gus Garcia Middle School in the mid 1980s. They then established an organized gang at Memorial High School in the Edgewood Independent School District. This high school is near St. Mary's University, a private Catholic college that draws students from throughout South Texas. The BTK/WSVK became the biggest age-graded street gang in San Antonio from about 1990 to 2000, with city-wide membership.

Gang "Nations" and the Chicago Influence

The BTKs, the Ambrose, and the 2-6 provide an interesting foray into key mechanisms involved in the spread of modern gang subculture and structure. When a local street gang adopts the name of a "nation" such as the Crips, the Bloods, or in this case, the Latin Kings, Ambrose, and 2-6, the implication is that they are a "set" of the larger gang. Whether such claims are true is a topic that has been debated in the street gang literature for several decades (e.g. Hagedorn 1988; Maxson, 1993). The most authoritative voices on the gang migration topic once found little support for its role in the spread of gangs over long distances (Maxson, Woods, and Klein, 1996; Waldorf, 1993), but others have since found that it *is* a significant cause of such gang proliferation, particularly in places with newly emerging gang problems (Knox et al., 1996; Moreno 2006; Tapia 2014; Yearwood and Rhyne, 2007).

Chicago's gang culture had an enormous impact on that of San Antonio. The Latin Kings had become so popular and so large in Chicago that by the 1960s, even Mexican American boys from San Antonio visiting or living with family there had joined the gang (Blackie, The Boys Club). While such gang connections between the two cities are logical, given the normative migration stream of Chicanos between them, it became most evident in San Antonio in the 1980s and '90s. According to a list kept by the SAPD gang unit, the BTKs and the WSV Kings were two of at least twenty-eight different Kings sets throughout the city in the 1990s. On the surface, the suggestion is that they are part of the Almighty Latin King and Queen (ALKQ) nation, which was originally a Puerto Rican gang formed in Chicago in the 1940s and still headquartered there (Brotherton and Barrios 2004).

Despite the impression its founders may have intended to give, San Antonio-based Kings sets have never convincingly had strong ties to the ALKQ nation in Chicago. If there once were direct ties, local groups quickly distinguished themselves from the Chicago group. San Antonio-based Kings are never referred to as *Latin* Kings, for example, but did and continue to use lots of the group's folklore, signs, colors, etc. (i.e. that of the "people" nation). While employed in a federally funded youth gang intervention project in San Antonio in the mid to late 1990s, this author heard rumors from both youth and police that major Kings "summits" were periodically held in San Antonio. The rumor was that Latin Kings leaders in Chicago came to San Antonio to hold large meetings with local leaders and ranking members.[73] While formal gang ties of the local Kings sets to Latin Kings in Chicago are dubious,[74] the network connection of local Ambrose and 2-6 sets to Chicago are thought to be real (Dyer 2015).[75]

One of the most notable rivalries among 1980s and '90s-era Chicano street gangs was that of the Klik versus the Klan. These were both very large groups with members spread throughout the city. Perhaps this rivalry was one of the most memorable because of the perceived social class division between the groups. The Klik had members throughout the long-standing barrios in the West and South Sides, mainly. The Klan's origins were in areas in the north-central and northwestern parts of the city that were traditionally more affluent. They were known for wearing designer clothes and helped to set a trend among San Antonio street gangsters for a certain look, which included baggy designer jeans, oversized polo shirts (untucked), and expensive steel-toe work boots. One might say the Klan were the more "preppy" of the two groups, but with many guns and a willingness to use them. The class distinction was probably more perception than reality, however, as by this stage in San Antonio's growth, HUD Section 8 and other low-income housing units began creating distinct pockets of poverty within larger middle-class neighborhoods (Montejano 2010). The Klan also grew city wide and later established sets in the barrio (e.g. Culebra Park Klan, West Side Klan).

Previous chapters profiled individuals who were central to the delinquent barrio network from the 1940s through 1960. By the 1990s, poverty, semi- and fully automatic gun availability, and gangster subculture in San Antonio had become so widespread that singling out individuals in this way for this modern era is perhaps futile. Instead, I list what I've found to be the most reputable Chicano gangs of the era, aside from those discussed above. I group them by periods of activity and by longevity, and indicate which street gangs had or have prison gang ties. These assessments are based on a gang's overall reputation, SAPD gang database information,[76] gang member and police interviews, and in some cases, visual inspection of graffiti in the gang's known turf.[77] Differences in my fieldwork information and that originating from a police database on

Table 1: San Antonio's Most Notorious Chicano Street Gangs 1990s-2015[79]

a.) 1950s Gangs That Are or Were Recently Still Active		
Varrio La Blanca (VLB) † #	Varrio Grey Eagle (VGE)*	Puro Varrio Kenwood (PVK)*
Rock Quarry (RQ) †	Victoria Courts Gangsters (VCG)/The Fellas*	Varrio Ghost Town (VGT)*

b.) Active through 2012-2015		
Brownleaf Posse (BLP)	The Wrecking Crew #	Insane Chicano Gangsters (ICG)
Fearless Brown Soldiers	Rosedale Park Kings (RPK)	Lincoln Court Kings (LCK)
Chicano Azteca Mob	Most Hated Boys (MHB)	Sureño Trece (SUR-13)
Authorized to Kill (A2K) #	Puro Violent Players	Bad Boy Gangsters (BBG)
SA Browns	2-6	Puro Brown
Rivas Street Kings (RSK)	Midnite Colors	Presa St. Gangsters

c.) Active through 2005		
Dawg Pound	Timberhill Kings	West Side Mirasol Thugs
Kings of Perfection (KOP)	True Players	West Side Posse
the KIN	Suicidal Locos	ND Posse
Tommy Boy Players	Artistic Criminals	Raiders
The Capping Krew	Valley Hi Thugs (VHT)	Valley Hi Mob (VHM)

d.) 1990s Only		
Latin Crime Mob	Crazy Mexican Artists	Tepa-13[80]
Mexican Posse	Carnales Por Vida (CPV)	Legion of Doom#

d.) 1990s Only		
Suicidal Force (SF)[81]	8-Ball Posse (a.k.a. "*Puro Ocho*") #	Lighter Shade of Brown Crips

e.) Other Notable Groups with Varying Lifespans		
Aztec Mob*	Hispanic Assassins*	True Brown Aztecas*
One Big *Familia* (OBF)*	Deep West Vandals (DWV)^	Grand Theft Auto (GTA)^
Latino Party Crew (LPC)*	Lynch Mob^	Astor St. *Necios* (ASN)^
Bud Smokers Only (BSO)*	Us Necios Love Violence (UNLV)^	Latino Thugs^
Los Azteca Kings^	Nothing But Trouble Boys^	McKinley Thugs^
Rainbow Hills Rowdies^	Puro Mexicano Kings^	Where Chaos Begins*
San Eduardo Thugs (a.k.a. "SET Crew") †		LA Boyz#
Always Violent/Vandalizing Unit (AVU) †		Chicanos Taking Over (CTO)*
Evil Blunting Assholes/Evil Bloodied Assassins (EBA)*		
Dark/Dope Minded Kriminals/Down Ass Latinos/Kriminals^		

* gang still exists   † active through ca. 2005   ^ dissipated in the 1990s   # has prison gang ties.

the active status of a gang is a potential source of error. Changes in gang names resulting from the group's preferences or external pressures on new cohorts to change also contributes to minor errors in the list.[78]

On Ethnicity and Modern Chicano Street Gang Subculture

Now classical theories of gang formation posit that its members are often social misfits (Cohen 1955; Short and Strodtbeck 1965). Poverty is a strong selection mechanism for gang membership (Eitle, Gunkel, and Van Gundy 2004; Greene and Pranis 2007; Klein 1995), and it is well known that US race-ethnic minorities are disproportionately poor. In most American cities, black and Latino youth are true numeric minorities. Thus, it follows that street gang formation in such places would embrace ethnic identity, as seen with the Midwestern groups, the Latin Kings, the Latin Counts, and the Spanish Cobras that formed in the 1940s and '50s for example. Chicano gang emergence is often said to be linked to the social dislocation that can result from poverty and discrimination (Bogardus 1943; Duran 2012; Mirande 1987; Montejano 2010; Moore 1978; Vigil 1988), so it is intuitive that these groups would organize on the basis of ethnicity and social class. They may even look to their poor, ethnic-minority status as a badge of resistance and pride (Sanchez-Jankowski 1991). Judging from the names attached to about one-third of the formidable antisocial groups listed in Table 1 above, this process is salient even in "majority-minority" cities like San Antonio.

Although there are elements of ethnic pride embedded in modern Chicano street gang subculture, the role of ethnicity in shaping the subculture in the urban Southwest is rife with contradiction. Gang-unit officers and other keen observers of these groups will agree that the street gang proliferation era ushered in a generic "gangsta" subculture that quickly became the dominant mind-set among gang youth. Many street-oriented young Chicanos began to mimic black street subcultures in terms of language use, music preference, and gang structure, by adopting the "nation" frameworks of the Crips and the Bloods (see Decker & Van Winkle, 1997) or of the Folk and People (Hagedorn 1988). There is ample evidence of this in the gang names adopted by many groups of this generation. In fact, because they far outnumber black youth in San Antonio, there are more Chicano youth claiming membership in Crips and Bloods sets (African American gangs with west-coast origins), than there are black youth who claim these sets. In the East Side ghetto areas especially, there are a number of Bloods and Crips sets that are of mixed race (e.g.; Drug Overthrowing Gangsters; Grape Street Watts [Crips]; Northwest Crips), and in the barrios, there are a number of all-Chicano Bloods and Crips sets. Some of the notable ones include the Bloodstone Villains; Original Crip Gangsters (OCG's), Southbound Gangsters (Bloods), La Raza Bloods, Latino Crips, Altadena Block Crips (South West set), Indian Creek Gangsters (Crips), and South Side Crips.

This development is one of the major subcultural changes identified by elderly research subjects in the study. The 1950s generation of barrio gang members expressed much resentment for the fact that today's barrio youth "are out of touch with their history and *cultura.*" The inability of many of today's gang youth to speak Spanish or even use the Chicano street slang of the barrio is viewed by the past generation as a travesty. That the youth adopt the ways and culture of another group, and one with whom the youth of the older generation has experienced much friction in correctional settings, is frowned upon. This is a sub-theme in the narrative that "respect has been lost," because not only have the basic cultural markers (language) been lost, but so too have the norms that once governed barrio rivalries.

The discussion in chapter 5 on norms that have changed over time referenced reckless, over-the-top violence in episodes of street gang conflict. My contention is that modern Chicano gangs not only mimic the black gangs' style, customs, music, and speech, but also their methods and patterns of violence. In the general population, Latinos are far less violent than blacks, showing levels that are rarely much higher than that of whites (Martinez 2014), and often even lower (e.g. Sampson et al. 2005). Elevated levels of violence are pathological in any community, but especially where such levels are traditionally among the lowest. There is thus tension between the community's old value systems of "respect for the barrio" on the one hand, and the need to one-up an enemy, to be daring, and to get a reputation for committing *loco,* violent acts on the other (see Valdez, Kaplan, and Codina 2000). Word travels fast about a *vato* (guy) who "goes *recio*" (hard/fast), which is something valued and honored by the gang subculture in general.[82] This is interesting to note as a "period" effect, because while this has always been the case in the ghetto and the barrio, the scale and the weaponry of the modern age makes violence qualitatively different from what occurred in the past. Importation of the hyper-violent subculture from Chicago and influence from the dominant black gang subculture seem to drive these effects among Chicanos.

Despite this, as a longstanding subculture in the community, there are also many strains of cultural preservation evidenced in today's Chicano gangs in San Antonio. Modern groups express ethnic pride and rally around it, as shown in the gang names listed above and in the ethnic-based gangs they form in correctional facilities. There are also conscious attempts by gang leaders to honor older barrio traditions and norms. For example, to the extent that prison and street gang operations are reciprocal in nature

(Valdez et al. 2009; Valdez and Enriquez 2011), there is regulation of street violence by prison gangs (Morrill 2007). These actions derive from the founding philosophy of most Chicano prison gangs, who view themselves as warriors for *la raza*, a people downtrodden by the dominant Anglo system in the United States. Prison gang members indoctrinate younger members of their families into this belief system, and important links are formed across the generations. For example there are "gang families" composed of a group of biological brothers, who make their mark on the barrio and are known to several generations of police and other gangs (e.g. Los Reyna de la Paloma [1940s and '50s]; Los Berlanga de la Lake [1950s and '60s]; Los Romo del Klik [1990's]).

Revisiting the Underclass Latino Debate

In considering the changes in San Antonio's Chicano gang subculture over time, I borrow from the underclass perspective that corresponds to the gang timeline described herein. In 1993, Joan Moore and Raquel Pinderhughes published an impactful book called *In the Barrios: Latinos and the Underclass Debate* that is relevant to the current discussion. It was an edited volume of studies on Latino poverty in several Southwestern and East Coast barrios. Various authors studied Chicago, Houston, Laredo, Brooklyn, LA, and Miami, profiling social and economic life in those places and including informal economies driven by drug and criminal subcultures. The general conclusion was that the underclass framework that fit the comparably poor, predominantly black population in the Midwest did not work well to analyze the plight of poor urban Latinos, especially in the Southwest. The underclass characteristics of poor Latino neighborhoods in the Texas study sites were culturally and behaviorally similar to that of blacks and Puerto Ricans in other regions, but their onset was not necessarily dictated by the same structural economic forces.

In one chapter, Nestor Rodriguez (1993) wrote that the constant in-migration of Mexicans to large Southwestern cities like Houston makes their poverty experience different from that of poor populations in other US regions. Recent Latino immigrants tend to harmoniously mix into established Chicano communities in the Southwest, which dilutes the otherwise negative effects of poverty at the community level, and makes the barrios there safer and richer in traditional Mexican culture. Valdez (1993) made a similar assessment for the border town of Laredo.

Whereas both authors described the gradual concentration of poverty in these cities over time, they did not attribute such changes to specific, cogent structural forces such as the Midwestern rustbelt conditions. Instead, the concentration of poverty into low-income government-funded housing projects and its negative impacts on less-affluent Southwestern communities seemed to be part of a wide-sweeping balkanization phenomenon that occurred in all US regions, prompted by flawed public housing policies and sheer city growth. One might simply refer to these as modernity effects. In both Texas cases, but especially in Laredo, poor Latinos adjust to high community-level rates of poverty by relying more on the informal economy, namely on the drug trade, which is abundant in this region. Although the drug addiction, sex work, criminal activity, and welfare dependency that is normally associated with underclass subculture is present in all US regions, drug trafficking and drug availability are more abundant in the Southwest, an important distinction from the Midwestern underclass scenario.

San Antonio is not only geographically positioned between Houston and Laredo (the two Texas cities analyzed in Moore and Pinderhughes 1993), it also represents a mix of the economies of both, and is the midway point in the drug trafficking route between the two places. While more specific structural causes of historical barrio violence in San Antonio are handled elsewhere (see Martinez 2014), a general hypothesis is that Chicano street youth devolved into the underclass over the last several decades for a host of policy reasons known as the "war on drugs" (Chambliss 1994), "the incarceration binge" (Western 2006), and the "school-to-prison pipeline" (Fabelo et al. 2011). These policy paradigms are shown to have disproportionately ensnared young, poor, minority males into the juvenile and criminal justice systems, further limiting their chances of success in life. For many, this helps to cement their fate as members of the underclass. Previous generations, too, had to deal with similar forms of discrimination—both the daily, interpersonal types and structural (policy-oriented) ones, but in terms of the latter, perhaps not on the same scale that modern Chicano youth do. As the underclass categorization is based on multiple generations of abject poverty and isolation from mainstream forms of social capital, among other things, perhaps the current generation has been hit the hardest by structural forces.

This discussion is focused on cultural shifts for Chicanos in the Southwest, but in the end, whether one focuses on rustbelt conditions in the Midwest or different types of structural economic shifts in the Southwest, the result for modern street gang subculture is now very similar across race and geography. We are in the age of the generic "gangsta" subculture that conditions every ethnic gang context in America, no matter how steeped in older, ethnic traditions those subcultures may be.

The Generic Gangsta Subculture and Chicano Barrio Gangs

In today's barrios, ghettos, and even in white poverty contexts, modern gang norms, subcultures, and behaviors most often embody a generic ghetto gangsta culture that transcends race and ethnicity. Perhaps due to media effects, black, white, Latino, Native American, and to some extent, even Asian street gang members of today all seem to have embraced the dominant underclass cultural norms of the ghetto. Martinez (2014) points to the nationwide appeal of the informal but booming crack cocaine market of the 1980s to ghetto and barrio youth. Its quick, lucrative profits represented a rational choice adjustment to shifts in the economy that left many of these youth few options for legitimate, gainful employment, and it was a central part of the gangsta image they craved.

The latest factor exacerbating these developments in street culture is the widespread access that even this class of individuals has to high-tech gadgets used in online social networking. These have increased connectivity with similar others, and they provide ready access to online entertainment and information that feeds into the underclass gangsta subculture. It is one that glorifies gang rivalry, violence, drug dealing, machismo, smoking "blunts" to remain high all day, and using the slang vernacular of the black ghetto, replete with its particular dialect. In short, it is heavily influenced by the images and messages of gangsta rap music, which became popular in the 1980s (Kubrin 2005). In thinking about the criminal class concepts introduced in chapter 1, whatever core theories one may use to describe the rapid escalation of underclass street crime in the modern age, there clearly are period effects that are not well accounted for in the current literature on street criminals or gang members. Here and in the past few chapters, I have simply referred to these as the effects of modernity, where poverty subcultures are strongly conditioned by race and ethnicity and criminal subcultures.

While the gangsta subculture that overtook America's underclass youth populations remains the dominant trope in the barrio, ethnicity still plays a convincing role in determining the particular form of a gang's identity. It is still a key factor in shaping gang intensity, longevity, structure, and networks. In terms of what types of youth or families are drawn into the gang subculture, Valdez (2005) makes the distinction between traditional and nontraditional Mexican American [Chicano] homes in San Antonio's barrios. Non-traditional households are those with lots of drug abuse and its collateral consequences of incarceration, female participation in sex work, welfare dependency, etc. (i.e., underclass characteristics). Traditional houscholds are essentially the working and middle class Chicano families. It follows that if youth from traditional Chicano homes experiment with the street gang subculture, they are apt to belong to more benign groups, and it is more likely to be a passing phase. These are the youth most likely to embrace the generic gangsta subculture that is widely available to America's youth via mass media, rap music, and so on. Kids from nontraditional Chicano homes are more likely to be part of hard-core, multigenerational Chicano gangs with links to adult criminal gangs. Whether a gang embraces old-school Chicano barrio values and mentality or a modern gangsta one is thus not a trivial or happenstance matter.

An interesting development in the traditional/non-traditional framework for San Antonio is the hybrid generation called Tango Orejon, whose history was provided in chapter 6. This group has one foot in the street-based gangsta subculture, and through their historical affiliation as a recruitment pool for Texas Latino prison gangs, the other foot in the hardcore underclass (i.e., "non-traditional") Chicano subculture that Valdez (2005) described. In addition to the rational actor sensibilities of this group discussed in chapter 6, the Tangos' split from the prison gang hierarchy is also a result of the modern gangsta codes they follow versus old-school Chicano gang codes.[83] Texas's Tango hybrid gangs are reckless groups who shirk the established order and hierarchy, which once provided respect to prison gang leaders and members. The Tangos' "power in numbers" approach to engaging in conflict with prison gangs requires that they recruit a broader range of youth, to include black and white youth who are part of the generic gangsta generation. While Tango O.G.s (now in their late thirties in age) may have deeper roots in San Antonio's Chicano gang subculture, many Tango members are relatively new to the game (i.e., first generation gangstas). By contrast, Chicano youth belonging to more stable, multigenerational gangs are more likely, for family and other values-based reasons, to still gravitate toward the traditional prison gang hierarchy.

Dissipating Networks, Honoring Traditions, and Hybrid Formations

The network of Chicano barrio delinquents, dope pushers, and users in San Antonio was identifiable and notably finite in the pre-1960s era. Growth of the barrio thinned out these connections significantly. In theory, growth of the subculture should result in higher quantified density of networks because of the possibility of more interconnections (Faust 2006). But the current reality of Chicano street gangs seems to show otherwise. In the 1970s, the Chicano civil rights movement supplanted much barrio gang activity among San Antonio's youth (Montejano 2010), further disrupting and perhaps dissipating the old barrio gang network (Martinez 2014). The 1980s saw a fierce return to barrio gang culture, but it came in such an intense and widespread manner that the phenomenon can only be explained by the conditions of modernity detailed throughout this chapter. These include the weakening of ethnic pride, gang migration, the social mimicry of black gangs, technological advances in weapons, transportation, and communication, and the growth of underclass conditions. If there is a new Chicano barrio gang network in place, it is only thinly based on past connections, if it is based on them at all ("Carlos," El Circle). A new order has been established in the barrio, and its ultra-violent methods prompted the youth of the early 1990s to follow suit with outrageous efforts to make names for themselves and their gangs. This reputation-seeking aspect of Chicano gang subculture is a constant over time, yet its modern manifestation appears to be qualitatively different from that of the past, partly because of changes in the tools of the trade. Easy and widespread access to vehicles, guns, drugs, and the increased number of targets that accompanied the proliferation of gangs all contributed to the violence spike in the early 1990s.

In this case study, outside influences—both geographic and cultural—seem to have changed the network structure of the barrio's delinquent groups. Yet despite the heavy influence of black and Puerto Rican youth gang structures and cultures on Chicanos in San Antonio and the Southwest, there is still evidence of efforts among Chicanos to honor longstanding traditions in local barrio gang history. The groups that embody ethnic pride in their gang name and norms seem to represent a distinct and quickly vanishing type of modern San Antonio barrio gangster. Whether their gang name is an ethnocentric one such as Chicanos Taking Over, or one that is tied to a specific micro locality, such as the Rivas Street Kings, the implication is that their barrios stand for something larger than themselves, in keeping with the Chicano barrio tradition. These gangs, especially the ones tied to a street name or locality, are perhaps the closest thing we have today to those archetypal barrio street corner groups of a bygone era. Ethnocentricity in a modern Chicano gang name suggests that the group has a political conscience that is influenced by older members of their families. Their value system also likely resembles the value system of the 1950s-era barrio gangsters that I studied.

Whether Chicano youth still form or sustain street-corner societies is a point of disagreement among my primary research subjects (the elders), current youth gang unit officers, current street gang members, and social commentators from other southwestern Chicano gang locales. The elders insist that modern gangs do not, in any way, resemble the turf gangs they formed in the 1950s. Seasoned youth gang officers refute this view, stating "sure, there are still plenty of places where if a rival gang member gets caught in the wrong turf area, they will get badly hurt or shot" (Castañola 2015). This is also the view of several current Chicano gang youth in San Antonio whom I interviewed about the topic.

Los Angeles-based journalist Sam Quinones (2014), however, wrote a piece for the *Pacific Standard* called "The End of Gangs," in which he compellingly argues that street gangs have disappeared from public view in Southern California. Here, again, the importance of studying Texas's Chicano street gangs apart from those in California is illustrated, but one must admit that Quinones's observation that old barrio gang hangouts are now clear of open congregating is becoming more of the norm throughout the Southwest. He notes that gentrification of inner city street corner gang hangouts and non-gang families again enjoying public parks represents the end of gangs as we once knew them. Indeed, implied in Quinones's thesis is that we are in a post-street-gang era that is largely driven by the use of communication technology, making it less necessary to engage in public loitering to conduct gang business.

Chicano Gangs and Ethnic Hybridization

Modern Chicano street gangs that mimic black gangs are an interesting hybrid to study. They emerge from some mechanism or combination of forces that is apparently not steeped in local Chicano tradition. In the case of the serious black-influenced Chicano gangs named earlier (e.g. Bloodstone Villains, Grape Street Watts), whatever their *raison d'être*—whether it be drug profits, armed robberies, attacking rivals, or whatever the solidarity-forming activities of the group are—they build hyper-violent traditions of their own, perhaps because they have to compete with the serious black gangs on San Antonio's East Side (e.g. the East Terrace Gangsters or the Wheatley Courts Gangsters). Some youths went this way simply because they grew up in the East Side, which now experiences ever more succession of blacks by Mexicans and Chicanos, and some racial tension as a result (Cancino et al. 2009). The irony is that while these East Side Chicano youth were influenced by the culture and value systems of the poor black youth in their midst, their older relatives were often members of Latino adult prison gangs, which affords them resources and makes them formidable groups. By contrast groups that mimic the black subculture but who do not have such a background to compete with black gangs can be simply understood as temporary, superficial formations with little history and low odds of a future as an organized group (see Yablonski's 1959 classical definition of such gang formations as "near groups"). In Texas, these are phenomenological urban formations whose members will likely turn *Tango* once they land in adult county jail for the first time after reaching the age of seventeen. Such groups are closely related to other more benign hybrid formations that always threaten to become "the real thing."

A final topic on hybridized subcultures in the current age of gang modernity is that of groups that approximate gangs, but are not gangs per se. These barrio subcultures include tagging crews (graffiti artists), party crews, dance crews, and car clubs. These groups are important insomuch as they help to define the scope of the "gang problem" in a given area, often being mistaken for genuine gangs, mostly because they resemble street gangs in many ways. Some of these groups in the roughest West Side San Antonio barrios have been forced to evolve into full-fledged gangs for protection from harassment by pre-existing gangs (Valdez, et al. 2009). In building a citywide gang database in the early 1990s, it became commonplace for any police gang unit, whether SAPD, the county sheriff, or local school district police, to photograph every suspected gang member they stopped and "blue sheet" them with a quick profile.[84] By the early 1990s, this resulted in documenting two thousand hard-core gang members in the city, equivalent to about 2 percent of the county's middle and high school students at that time (Duff 1994). There were some 2,500 associates exhibiting less violent behavior that were also documented in this early stage of the database's existence.

The tagging crews and party crews, especially, engage in activities that are also typical of street gang behavior. Graffiti as a form of artistic expression is seldom distinguished from gang-related graffiti by members of law enforcement or the general public. Taggers also often dress like and carry themselves with an inner-city street-kid posturing that resembles that of the gang youth. They also often abuse the same types of drugs and pursue the same girls as gang youth (Valdez 2007). The gang and tagger subcultures are so similar in San Antonio that both researchers and gang unit officers refer to those that appear to be involved in both types of activities as "tag-bangers" (Valdez et al. 2009). Several of these groups made the list of serious Chicano gangs offered in this chapter, such as the Artistic Criminals, Crazy Mexican Artists, and the Puro Mexicano Kings. The Latino Party Crew and the Shut 'Em Down car club were also reputable 1990s groups that gradually became involved in gang violence over time.

Summary

This chapter profiled the modern Chicano street gang in San Antonio and its place in the broader historical timeline of the urban barrio gang phenomenon. It illustrates what we know about the prevalence of these formations, how we measure gang violence and other gang-related crimes, and how gangs became a local youth epidemic. In this regard, knowledge of barrio gangs, while better now than ever before, is still quite elusive. The police lens provides useful information about their prevalence and intensity, but police data systems are not very reliable. Different law enforcement and supervision agencies seem to address different parts of the issue. Here, I am in agreement with Curry (2000) that law enforcement information greatly overlaps with but does not fully match the academic research findings on these groups.

Documenting the most active, dangerous, and therefore reputable Chicano gangs in modern-day San Antonio served to illustrate several facets of the subculture. It addresses a central question about barrio longevity and examines the process of continuity. Not counting the resurrection of the infamous Ghost Town gang documented in chapter 3, or the evolution of El Con to the LA Boyz in this chapter, there are five barrio gangs that date back to the 1950s that were still recently active in San Antonio, giving more definitive evidence of some fifty to sixty years of continuity. The role of social class (even if only perceived differences) in the Klik versus Klan rivalry was an unexpected finding. The continued importance of ethnicity in shaping gang identity was evident in one-third of modern gang names, which seems to reflect the intergenerational tension seen between groups espousing a gangsta identity over Chicano pride. Traditionalism appears to be fledgling, but it is not altogether gone. Finally, the links between Chicano street and prison gangs is made more explicit, showing which San Antonio groups were known to be fully co-opted by the adult gangs. The tie between the street and prison gangs is far understated here, however. As described in chapter 6, street gangs are a training ground of sorts for the prison gangs to recruit from, mainly on an individual basis, according to the youth's reputation, family ties, etc.

Picking up on the topic of Chicano gang modernity introduced in chapter 6, this chapter relates it to youth street gangs, coming full circle with the book's central theme. The importation of well-organized gang nation structures from Chicago and LA served to make the 1990s version of the phenomenon a popular craze locally. This disrupted the traditional barrio gang network structure and its cultural norms, and escalated gang violence to an unprecedented level. As with adult prison gangs, this level of violence shocks the sensibility of a Chicano community that has historically had lower levels of lethal violence citywide (Martinez 2014), and the behavior is therefore unsustainable. As hypothesized in earlier chapters, the size of the network (if it might still be referred to as such) starts to matter. The sheer prevalence of participation and the widespread access to weapons, driven by the compelling influence of gangsta rap on impressionable youth, are aspects of modernity that transformed the Chicano barrio gang subculture into a genuine social problem. Prior to the introduction of these elements, the subculture was every bit as intense, but not prevalent enough, nor equipped with the same tools as modern youth, to drive the citywide violence rate up to such an alarming level (Martinez 2014).

Eight

Lessons from Analyzing Chicano Gang Formations over Time

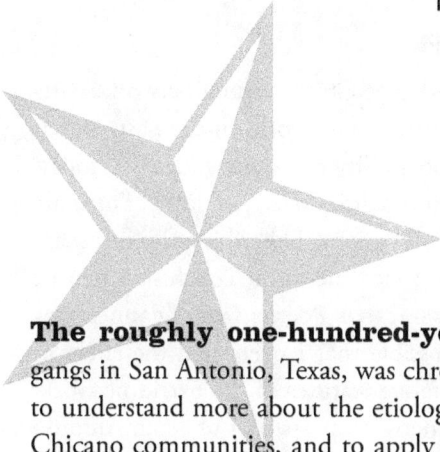

The roughly one-hundred-year history of Chicano barrio gangs in San Antonio, Texas, was chronicled in this study. The goal was to understand more about the etiology of criminal street subcultures in Chicano communities, and to apply the knowledge to big cities in the southwest generally. Delinquent subcultures are a durable aspect of social life in these communities; thus the Chicano case has long been a significant part of the country's criminological landscape. Yet in mainstream crime research there is only sparse information about the various forms these groups take over time, their longevity, intergenerational conflicts, and other politics.

The case of southern California has dominated the sociological research on barrio gangs, but not much has been written on the rich history of these formations in Texas. This study drew heavily on the notable exceptions of Montejano (2010), and of Avelardo Valdez and co-authors (1999; 2004; 2005; 2007; 2009), who delivered much useful information on the subject. By tracking the evolution of modern urban barrio networks in San Antonio, my aim was to more comprehensively fill this gap in the literature.

This critical examination of the barrio gang as a neighborhood-based social institution brought new insights about a social phenomenon once thought to be rather normative in the vast Chicano sectors of San Antonio. Using varied anthropological research methods led me to many surprising findings about the basic nature of this type of formation and about the individuals that were drawn to it (if not selected into it). There were essentially two main research objectives at the heart of the book. The first dealt with the barrio's network structure and the second dealt with the content of the character of barrio dwellers over time.

Depicting Barrio Networks

A primary focus of the book is to depict Chicano gang network structure. The book gives ample description of networks of the past, and at every opportunity, I evaluated the possibility that a network exists today. What, if any, are the network commonalities over the years? There are several hypotheses and potential implications. Describing the finite nature of the 1950s barrio gang universe led me to the conclusion that its network parameters were restricted and that a dense web of connections existed within it. However, it is possible that I overstated the effect of scale on the density or other qualitative features of the barrio network. This would suggest that the social network properties of a San Antonio Chicano gang universe of approximately 1,300 individuals in the 1950s are similar to those of one having some 5,000 individuals in the modern era (in 2007, by the study's data).

Another possibility is that in a large, high-poverty city like San Antonio, participation in street life is so common in the barrio that in any era, it is difficult to discern an underlying social network of participants, let alone depict its structure. Armed with retrospective data for the 1950s, I assumed that it *was* possible and made my best attempt to qualitatively describe the network. It is up to the reader to decide if this was accomplished. If not, it could imply that despite the different size of the Chicano gang population in both eras, the subjective, lived experience of the gang milieu may be comparable. In other words, to those who lived through the 1950s era, it may have seemed that a very large universe of youth participated in street life, and that it was not as small or finite as I suggest. Very few research subjects were forceful with their responses to this question, but it was intuitive to all that smaller is denser in the case of Chicano barrio networks.

A final possibility is that there is a decipherable network in both eras, and both networks are dense. If Chicano gang networks are familial, neighborhood and prison based, and limited to proven, respected members of the barrio street scene, then we might expect for them to resemble each other regardless of scale. Given the findings regarding the consistency of the proportion of gang-involved youth in both eras, there are sure to be underlying similarities in 1950s and modern barrio network structure. Moreover, while difficult to measure, the technological advances in communication and social networking may increase the density of modern gang networks to compensate for the larger scale.

Human Capital in Chicano Gangs and the Underclass Debate

A second underlying theme in this book is related to gang members as an underclass population. In depicting the early stages of the subculture, I was surprised to encounter an eclectic spectrum of 1950s barrio gang members who led very interesting lives that did not correspond with our current understanding of the trajectories of underclass subjects. It is possible that the men in their seventies and eighties who participated in the study represented a subset of barrio gang youth with higher levels of self control, IQ, social capital, and so on. But even this was ruled out as a research limitation, because these subjects spoke of the lives of other barrio gang youth who did not survive this long into adulthood as persons with normative and often remarkable character, resources, family members, life experiences, and contributions to the community. I am therefore confident that I accurately captured this facet of the their collective subculture and constitution as a cohort.

In chapter 3, I claim that aside from the obvious factors of poverty, ethnic minority status, and in some cases, drug use, attempts to predict 1950s era Chicano barrio gang membership presented a "black box" for criminology. That is, given the high rate of Chicano youth poverty in San Antonio (Chambers 1940; Marquez et al. 2007; Montejano 2010), it cannot realistically be considered a risk factor for gang involvement, and therefore gang selection mechanisms are poorly understood. In part, the study's methodological circumstances enabled me to draw such a conclusion. The finite network structure of this subculture that I focused upon—from the 1940s to the 1970s—was fortuitous in this regard. These parameters allowed me to probe the lives of a sizeable, reputable segment of the overall barrio gang universe in such detail that intriguing, counterintuitive facets of their lives and families became apparent. Without data on the biological or psychological indicators thought to select youth into delinquency (and the role of these factors is questionable at best), gang youth profiles and life outcomes are nearly indistinguishable from those of poor, non-gang Chicano youth. I cannot as confidently make the same claim for members of the modern Chicano gang subculture in San Antonio because it is methodologically not feasible to follow the same approach for the relevant groups of today. Absolute population growth and the relative growth of this seemingly underclass population preclude any replication options.

Several issues brought to light in chapter 6 do allow me to comment on this topic for the modern context, however. From those insights, one could make a similar black box claim about modern Chicano barrio dwellers by noting that for two extremes—prison gang members (i.e., the elite of the barrio street crime world) and the "losers" in this context both have experienced similar underclass living conditions as youth. In terms of the kinds of families and contexts they were born into, prison gang members are not a more privileged bunch than any other underclass barrio dweller. Indeed, it is *because* the prison gang member is too familiar with the most difficult hardships the barrio can offer that they are "the real thing" in terms of resource deprivation, exposure to violence and drug abuse, family dysfunction, etc.

Prison gang members have accrued specific knowledge about the rough-cut norms and illicit means of the barrio underclass, and it is something that cannot be feigned. In terms of where they started in life, these individuals are nearly indistinguishable from the drug-addicted, homeless Chicano who is unable to navigate the barrio social sphere to excel in it the way the *merecido* (prison gang member) has. The domain that the cognitive scientists call IQ seems the obvious choice for differentiation, but given that it best measures a grasp of concepts taught in or at least consistent with excelling in the American public school system (Isen 2010), we can't be sure of its utility here; most Chicano gangsters are school dropouts. The developmental, life-course criminologists propose hypotheses regarding life trajectory and predicting gang membership, but their "precocious transitions" concepts and other pivotal life events seem too idiosyncratic to individuals to be truly systematic in their application to broad population segments. Moreover, given all that was discovered in chapter 6 about varying levels of delinquent and criminal embeddedness, and how one arrives there, the life-course explanations are too simplistic to be of much utility.

For all of these reasons, I gave the most attention to *group-level* barrio dynamics in this study. While changes in these street-based criminal subcultures are well documented here, fundamental changes in human nature over time, or at least in the nature of the typical barrio dweller, are not well depicted. I admittedly vacillated on this issue of whether levels of human capital have declined among the Chicano gang population over time. It is easy to dismiss today's gang-involved ghetto and barrio youth as desensitized "super-predators" (DiIullio 1995) produced by degraded gene pools, violence norms in the family and in society, and so on. However, in light of falling delinquency rates since the 1990s, predictions about the mass devolution of gang youth into sociopathic behavior have clearly been misguided. Still, whether gang youth have become devalued in their potential to contribute to their families, the community, and society is a difficult research question to address. Clearly, their levels of social capital, by definition, have dropped off in a society growing in absolute size and complexity, but we hold out hope that this can be remedied with favorable community structure and other informal control mechanisms that manifest within the nuclear and extended family.

Studying Group and Community-Level Processes

Where humans need the group collectivity to thrive, à la Maslow's hierarchy of needs, and gangs are by definition groups, questions asked at the individual level are probably minimally important for the subdiscipline of criminology addressing gang studies. Findings among the growing group of quantitative gang studies that take individuals as the unit of measurement have not borne much new information in the past few decades. They are also less useful in devising public policies to counter the social ills of gang life than those addressing group processes at the gang, community, or societal levels. This study found that structural features created some discontinuity in barrio traditions from the 1950s to the 1960s, which appeared to be a decade of change and reorganization of inner-city barrio structures to some degree. New groups emerged in San Antonio as poverty and discrimination intensified and barrio subcultures proliferated (Montejano 2010). As for modern manifestations of this trend, the shorter lifespan of gangs that form today suggest that these are a fad for many poor youth who have widespread access to a superficial gangsta subculture, compared to gangs that were based on family, community, ethnic pride, and other meaningful traditions.

Findings related to barrio longevity demonstrate that like the California model, the trend toward more ephemeral associations is also evident in San Antonio. The discontinuity of most of the oldest inner-city groups was attributable to urban redesign and the expansion of communities outward from the city's core. Several gangs established in the inner West Side in the early 1950s still exist today, however, and there is a need for more understanding of what types of barrio gangs experience such longevity or what contextual and other conditions create it. For street gang interventionists, it is conceivably more effective to deal with multiple generations of members of the gang to eradicate community problems than to chase around short-lived, volatile, single-generation groups that are primarily organized around delinquency. The example toward the end of chapter 2 of Ghost Town's evolution to Bad Company and back to Ghost Town over fifty years since the gang first emerged is also an interesting case that so far eludes a compelling analytical framework. Coupled with findings from chapter 7 regarding the stubbornness of ethnocentricity in modern barrio gang culture, it suggests that some of today's Chicano gang youth still value old barrio traditions, but they are in the minority and may soon be extinct.

Countervailing the preservation of barrio tradition and winning out in that community's ideological struggle are the external influences of gang migration and racial cross-pollination of once-identifiable Chicano gang norms. These factors have disrupted and likely forever altered any semblance of barrio gang networks as they were once known. Chapter 7 described an environment in 1990s San Antonio that was saturated with youth gang violence and culture. In that decade there was a critical mass of armed youth in the community with something to prove, creating an uncontrolled, unstructured context for violence to erupt at random. In such a setting, it was common for strangers to cross paths and have violent confrontations based merely on the color of the clothes they wore.

To be fair, American street gang subculture has always included engaging in violent conflicts with unknown others in turf battles, for thrills, machismo, and to uphold other elements of the decades-old street code (Sanchez-Jankowski 1991). Even in the 1950s, barrio gang processes were shown to be intense and based on these street codes. In those days, however, youth gang violence was more structured because the main organizing principle was the micro-unit of urban space. Recent work on

open-air drug markets controlled by street gangs shows that when portions of the inner city representing gang turf are clearly demarcated and
well understood by all players, violence tends to remain organized and
thus, minimized (Hughes 2013; Pappachristos 2013; Vargas 2014).

Study Conclusion

Inasmuch as participation in street violence, drug selling, and other parts
of the informal economy are functional adaptations to the social structure, the forces propelling Chicano gangs to exist are not temporary social phenomena. The gang context in major Chicano population centers
has lengthy historical bases rooted in weak opportunity structures, oppression, and discrimination, as illustrated in the literature for San Antonio (Montejano 2010), El Paso (Campbell 2009), Los Angeles (Mirandé
1987; Moore 1978; Vigil 1988), and Denver (Duran 2012), to name a
few. This study of San Antonio represents the most comprehensive case
study of barrio group organizational dynamics in a major Texas city to
date. With the exception of El Paso, no other Texas city is so conducive
to such historical exploration. Valdez (2005), for example, noted that
heroin has been the signature drug of choice among Chicano addicts
(tecatos) in San Antonio and South Texas's barrios for nearly a century.
This was evident in tracing the ecological roots of the barrio gang phenomenon to the Bounds, where heroin was first introduced to the city in
the 1920s (McKinney 1975).

Consistent with classical social disorganization theory, these delinquent traditions and connections persisted over time in inner-city San
Antonio. In every era studied, barrio gang youth appeared to have high
levels of commitment to their delinquent lifestyle. In the full century that
was examined here, it was evident that the barrio gang as a neighborhood
social institution has been an important organizing mechanism for a sizeable segment of poor Chicano youth. There were, however, important
changes in the institution over time. This study's findings suggest there
are period effects that are not well accounted for in current literature on
street criminals or gang members.

One fact that compels the broad characterization of the modern Chicano gang population as members of the underclass is the widespread
monolithic gangsta subculture that is predominant in the barrio today.
Due to gang migration and media effects, black, white, and most Latino

street gang members of today all seem to have embraced the underclass cultural norms of the black ghetto. The latest twist in these developments in street culture is the widespread access that youth have to high-tech social networking gadgets. It has increased connectivity with similar others and provides ready access to online entertainment and information that feeds into the underclass gangsta subculture described in chapter 7. The final assessment is that the age of modernity has impacted barrio youth community structure in meaningful and perhaps irreversible ways. Whether this is viewed in terms of (or attributed to) macro-economic restructuring, changes in delinquent subculture away from ethnocentricity, or fundamental changes in the levels of human capital of poor barrio youth, things appear to have changed more than they have tended to stay the same.

Appendix A
San Antonio's Barrio Gangs, 1940s and 1950s

Downtown-West

1. El Town
2. Los Cocos
3. Columbus
4. La Paloma (Alley)
5. El Boys Club
6. Los Bounds
7. El Wesley
8. Riverside
9. Victoria Courts
10. Garfield Alley
11. El Red Light (shoeshine stand)
12. Los Gallos
13. Las Americas
14. Moonglow
15. Butterfly
16. La Fortuna

West Side

1. El Con
2. Alazan Courts
3. El Gaucho
4. La India
5. Espiga
6. La Tripa
7. La Blanca
8. Cassianos (Courts)
10. El Alto
11. Ghost Town
12. The Lake
13. El Charco

14. Los Bradys (Courts)
15. Mirasoles (Courts)
16. Las Colonias
17. Los Luckeys (Locketts)
18. Calle Barclay
19. Los Black Cats
20. House of Neighborly Services
21. El Jalisco
22. Menchaca Homes
23. Calle Guadalupe

South Side

1. El Circle
2. La Dot
3. La Mission
4. Varrio Palo Alto
5. Varrio Grey Eagle
6. Taco Village
7. St. Henry's

North Side

1. Varrio Kenwood
2. La Loma (Rattlesnake Hill)
3. La Piedrera
4. La Botica (Olmos Park)
5. La Rosita
6. Lynwood gang

East Side

1. La Calle Austin
2. The East-End (Calle Porter)

San Antonio 1950s Barrio Nicknames

Al Capone	Chale (Los Cocos)	Cuate
Aleman	Chambon	Cucaracho
Auggie	Chancho	Cuyo
Baboo	Changa	Daddy O
Baby (El Circle)	Changuito	Dandy
Baby (Ghost Town)	Chanklas	Dangerous Dan
Baby (Las Colonias)	Chapote	Danny Bravo
Bacho	Chavalo	De la Madre
Bay	Cheche	Deeply
Beaver	Chendo	Diablito
Bebe	Chi-boy	Dimas
Bee-Bop	Chiboom	Dracula
Beto	Chimilio	Dragnet
Bibin	Chino	Dynamite
Big Light	Chino (El Circle)	El 35
Bimbo	Chino (La Paloma)	El Abel
Birdie (Alazan Courts)	Chiva	El Apache
Birdie (El Circle)	Chivo	El Archie
Blackie (El Boys Club)	Chocha	El Babe
Blackie (El Circle)	Choco	El Bebito
Blackie (Espiga)	Chocolate	El Bigotes
Blackie (La Dot)	Chon	El Black Diamond
Blackie Juanes	Chona	El Blanco
Bobo	Chota	El Bonne
Bolio	Chuy (Alazan Courts)	El Boogie
Bones	Chuyano	El Borracho
Borrado	Cobra	El Borrado
Boston Blackie	Coche	El Brujo
Buckwheat	Cogito	El Califas
Caballo	Colorado	El Canele
Calido	Columpio	El Canoso
Califas	Conejo	El Chanklin
Calvo	Cool John	El Chicken
Camote	Coque	El Chivo
Cantina	Cowboy	El Chore (El Boys Club)
Capone	Coyote	El Chore (El Town)
Chacho	Crucitas	El Chueco (Los Cocos)
Chale (Las Colonias)	Cuadrado	El Chueco (Taco Village)

El Chunga
El Chuno
El Cirjuelo
El Columpio (Alazan Courts)
El Comanche
El Congo
El Copeton
El Cucaracho
El Cuckeno
El Curly
El Diablo
El Diente
El Dormido
El Eskimbo
El Especk
El Fito
El Flash
El Floppers
El Galleta
El Gallina
El Gasofo
El Giraffa
El Giraffa (Las Colonias)
El Gordo
El Gorila
El Gorrilon
El Grifo
El Guzano
El Heavy
El Heavy (Victoria Courts)
El Huevo
El Indio
El Jerita
El Jerry Cheese
El Jiggies
El John Wayne
El Joiso
El Joka (El Alto)
El Joka (El Con)
El Joka (Shoe-Shine Stand)
El Joka (Taco Village)
El Kila
El Killer

El Laganias
El Leon
El Ma'gue
El Mando
El Marranito
El Mayate
El Melo
El Melodias
El Meme
El Mighty
El Monstro
El Morado
El Movie
El Moy (Los Cocos)
El Muerto
El Mula
El Mysterio
El Nene
El Pa'le
El Pajaro
El Panther
El Panzon
El Pelon (Las Colonias)
El Pelon (Los Cocos)
El Peludo
El Pepino
El Perro (Columbus)
El Perro (Los Cocos)
El Picon
El Piloto
El Pin
El Platano
El Pollito
El Ponka
El Poya
El Prieto
El Private
El Professor
El Queso
El Rainbow
El Rocky
El Salvador
El Sapos
El Sombra
El Tannis

El Tecato (Boys Club)
El Tecato (El Circle)
El Tigre
El Toronja
El Tortuga
El Tostado
El Train
El Viejo
El Wango
El Wero
El Yepo
Equinkle
Euwie
Fish
Fito
Flaco
Frog
Gabbo
Gangster
Hamburger
Heckle & Jeckle
Herbie
Ito
Japo
Jinga
Jingos
Joga
Joker
Joyo
Jungi
Junkito
Kiddo
Kike
Kiki
Kiko
Kino
La Carrucha
La Changa
La Mascota
La Mula
La Rata
La Wifa
Lagartijo
Lefty
Licho

Lil' Bit
Lito
Little Joe
Little Joe (Riverside)
Little Rudy
Los Camarones
Los Mercados
Los Rubios
Lupillo
Lupon
Manotas
Maqua
Marijuano
Maxis
Mayito
McCain
Mighty Mouse
Mikito
Mingo
Mocha
Mon
Moy (El Town)
Muco
Muerto (El Circle)
Muletas
Mun
Nacho
Navo
Nayo
Nixon
One-Eyed Gus
Ormiga
Papache
Parakeet
Pato
Paton
Paton (Las Colonias)
Payaso
Pebo
Pecas
Pee-wee
Pee-wee (Las Colonias)
Pepino (Alazan Courts)
Perico
Piano

Pilinga (Alazan Courts)
Pilinga (La Dot)
Pingo
Pino
Pitina
Piwa
Plastic
Polkas
Poninas
Ponka
Popo
Poyo
Quino
Rabbit
Rana
Raton (El Boys Club)
Raton (La Paloma)
Red
Reno
Ringo
Robe
Rock n Roll
Rolando
Ronia
San Anto
Sancos
Sapo (Las Colonias)
Scorpion
Shay
Shepe
Shia
Sin Cejas
Sorra
Spider
Supercat
Taco
Tete
Tex (Los Cocos)
Tex (Taco Village)
The Terror
Tiny
Tomate
Torpedo
Toto
Trine

Trocka
Trockita
Tury
Uncs
Urbano
Vache
Vakita
Venado
Venena
Vicho
Vore
Wawo
Wero
Wheaties
Wimpy
Wino
Zorra (El Circle)
Zorra (Las Colonias)
Zorro

Females:
Audrey
Bartola
Borrada
Chavela
Chayo
Gloria la prieta
Hope
Kika
La Agapita
La Boogie
La Chore
La Gatita
La George Washington
La Muneca
La Prieta
La Tiger
Lupe Luna
Matilde
Oralia
Ruth
Sara Perales
Teresa Brown

Appendix C
Jargon of the 1950s Era in San Antonio's Barrios[85]

Term or Phrase	Translation & Meaning	Notes
Mentado	Reputable; Well-known person	A known, respected person
Búle	Someone who is feared or who can fight or hold their ground	Variants are "*Un vato que le pone*" or "*Vato que no se aguite*"
Gorriliar; Gorrilón	To Intimidate/Threaten; A Bully	Going on the offensive and winning the fight or getting what one wants by force.
Blofiar	To bluff	
Hikiar	To rob someone of their drugs, money or other valuables	
Hacer un pare	Do a robbery	
Una Boogla	To do a burglary	A known burglar was also referred to as a *boogla*.
Chacharas	"Stuff"; often connotes stolen goods	In the prison culture, also the items one accumulates in one's "house" or cell.
La hóspita	The hospital; a salient location for gang boys and their families	Typically, Robert B. Green Hospital on the edge of the Bounds near the Riverside and Columbus barrios.
Shootiando	Legitimately selling goods (usually fruit) on the roadside	These vendors are a vital source of info as "eyes & ears" of the barrio.

continued

Term or Phrase	Translation & Meaning	Notes
La Fédica /*Férickal*	Fredericksburg Road	Main avenue from northwest downtown outward to suburbs.
Motocyca	Motorcycle	
Terkiar	Forcibly impose something	"*Terko*" = Stubborn
Timba/Gorra	Small capsule/balloon of heroin	
Tirar	Inject (shoot up) drugs	
Carabina	Syringe; also, a type of gun.	A *carabina* (syringe) is also known as an "*erre.*" Illegal possession of one in the late 1950s or early 1960s often resulted in a lengthy prison sentence.
Seca	Downer / Barbiturate	Makes one's mouth dry (*seco*)
Esquadra	Non-gang member / non-drug user	A square or straight person
Dale Courte	Rough 'em up to join the gang or to discipline for violating the gang's street code.	Akin to "*se rajo*" (backed down) or "*se hizo patras*" *en un* (backed out of a) gang fight
Ensalada	To disrespectfully take someone's shoes or other items	An older version of "punking someone out."
Quitarle los calcos	To "take someone's shoes"	Could be an actual robbery, or a a jocular threat, as in asking an associate "What size are your shoes?" for example.
Pleito casado	Serious rivalry	Automatic violent encounter on site.
Guitarra	The "top dog" in a gang	
De pura Barba	For the hell of it	Doing something bad to someone for no good reason

Chotiar	To shoot someone down	Burst their bubble
Numero	A con or a fake	To put one over or deceive
Tapita	Barrio Pachuco hat	Brim-hat
Alambre	Wire; the rumor mill	Generically: communication
Alambre chueco	Crooked wire	False or incorrect information
Stacies *(i.e. Los Estacies)*	Stacy Adams dress shoes	Sold at *Joske's / Penners* department stores in San Antonio
Trae Corrido/Chaqueta	*"Un Relaje"* A Snitch / Informant	Or that the person has a *chaqueta* (jacket) that makes him unreliable, unwanted; having a socially undesirable char-acteristic or reputation
Rueda	A "high roller" or "baller"	Mid-level to higher level drug dealer
El Condado (i.e. "The County")	The County Jail	The most salient for the current study is the "old" county jail on Camaron Street, until 1962 when the new facility went up. There are several urban tales about the old jail that include worthless guard dogs and a secret escape route.
Una Sopa	A prison sentence	Amount of time; e.g. "una sopa de 10 years."
El uno	Harlem Unit I	Texas Prison System Unit
El dos	Harlem Unit II	Texas Prison System Unit
El once	Ft. Leavenworth Federal Penitentiary.	ónce = Eleven i.e. "LEVENworth"
El jamón	Eastham Unit, Texas Prisons	*Jamón* = ham

continued

Term or Phrase	Translation & Meaning	Notes
Cadena	To arrive at a prison	Modern usage: To be transferred into/out of a prison facility
Safanar	To leave prison	
Marrano	A security trustee	Building "Tender" system in the Texas Department of Corrections.
Melasa	Jailguard / prison guard	
Tacuche	Lawsuit	A suit and tie or a zoot suit.
"Se te cae el canton"	"Your house will fall/ crumble"	One's plot goes wrong or one meets with misfortune

Notes

1. For example, in May 2014, a San Antonio-area police officer with no criminal history who was ambushed and murdered by masked gunmen was later found to be an associate of the notorious Texas Mexican Mafia (Contreras 2014).

2. Some of the most infamous were *Ghost Town, El Circle, La Dot,* and *Varrio Grey Eagle,* to name a few.

3. Roy Valdez, a longtime gang-intervention social worker with the Good Samaritan social services center deep in the heart of the gang and crime-ridden West Side of San Antonio wrote several unpublished but insightful manuscripts on Chicano gang warfare in the 1950s and 1960s. Otherwise, organized material on barrio gangs of this era is scarce.

4. The existence of Chicano gangs is often conceptualized as an outgrowth of social inequality and injustice (Mirande' 1987; Montejano 2010; and Duran 2012).

5. The focus of chapters 6 and 7 of this book.

6. In following the lives of a large group of men to age seventy, Laub and Sampson (2003) find that delinquents have a much higher mortality rate than non-delinquents. General life expectancy tables for this demographic also show the exigency of data collection before the opportunity is lost to mortality (US Census Bureau 2012).

7. Several local news stories profiling the research project generated public interest and subject referrals, requiring some screening by the author and other subjects.

8. Appendix A contains a list of all 1940s and 1950s-era San Antonio Barrio Gangs.

9. Appendix B contains a list of all street names encountered in the study. This exercise takes a page from the sociolinguistic perspective to gauge whether barrio gang street names tend to change in character over time. Observed similarities would signal cultural preservation or emulation within this social (street) institution. Differences may be attributed to shifting preferences in youth subculture (i.e., modernity).

10. This is the most recent, reliable data year available. In this author's opinion, significant changes in the structure of the SAPD gang unit and other specialized police units that inform the database after 2007 have compromised the integrity of the data. Having studied the database since that time, many errors in gang names and other inconsistencies are apparent, suggesting that recent lists are not as reliable as those from 2007 and years prior. More on this in chapter 7.

11. Federal statute (28 CFR, part 23), and Texas Code of Criminal Procedure Chapter 61, require removal of a person from the active gang database if he or she does not re-offend within a two-year timeframe for juveniles and five years for adults. Most agencies (SAPD included) will place these cases in an inactive file unless or until a new offense is recorded. The active gang database therefore offers a reasonable snapshot of the number of active gang offenders at any given time (validity issues with the contents of the database aside).

12. It is reasonable to assume that a police-generated gang database will provide a close match to one generated via peer nomination by gang members. The only study that shows any dissimilarity in police versus subject-generated lists is Curry (2000), which compared names of self-reported gang members in two Chicago middle schools to a police-held gang list for that area of the city. This is quite a different research context from this study, however, as the former is plagued by the inherent errors in self-reported youth data. These include both exaggeration and false information given by gang wannabe youth, and deception by serious gang offenders who are coached by older gang members not to reveal their gang ties.

13. One of the oldest San Antonio juvenile street gangs to be documented in print (no ethnicity information offered) were the Club Boys, identified by city detectives as a group "ranging in age from 11-14 in the Downtown section" in a 1920 *San Antonio Evening News* newspaper story. Two other boy gangs referenced in the article were an unnamed group from the Government Hill area and an unnamed group specializing in burglaries around the city. Ethnicity information was not offered for these groups either.

14. Migration of Mexican American families to and from Chicago is a recurrent theme in this study's data. There is a very strong connection between San Antonio and Chicago in terms of familial-based barrio networks. In the 1950s and 1960s both LA and Chicago-based barrio gang members often referred to San Antonio as "Little Chicago" ("El Mysterio" [*El Alto & El Circle]* and "Blackie" [*Boys Club]*). The migration of Chicano families between these cities is evident in normative life, but is especially salient in the street gang subculture. One example is a barrio gang called "El Chicago" in West Side San Antonio (The Villa Veramendi Housing Projects) in the early 1960s (Montejano 2010; Valdez n.d.). Another example is the profound migration/transmission of "Folk" and "People" nation gang affiliations into the San Antonio Chicano juvenile street gang subculture from Chicago in the 1980s and 1990s, a topic that is detailed in chapter 7.

15. Ironically, in a 1940 newspaper article, a prominent juvenile judge, Charles Anderson touted the Boys Club as such an effective agency in combating delinquency that none of the 1,200 boys that officially registered as its clients in its first 18 months of existence had ever come before the juvenile court (*San Antonio Express-News* 1940).

16. A likely predecessor to the 1970s-1990s group "The Town Freaks." (See Casillas 1994).

17. As this area is also adjacent to Rattlesnake Hill, a.k.a. Government Hill, it is likely these are a subsequent cohort/generation of the group referenced by city detectives in a 1920 *San Antonio Evening News* article.

18. Ghost Town, Los Courts, El Circle; La Dot, Varrio Grey Eagle, and Varrio Palo Alto.

19. Recent gang violence in Chicago provides an example of how the reorganization of long-established neighborhoods with the demolition of large public housing projects can result in the redistribution of gangs to new areas, and turf conflicts can begin anew (Young 2012). After the demise of the Bounds in the late 1950s, this reoccurred in San Antonio with the closure of the inner-South Side Victoria Courts housing project in year 2000, a 660-unit project with a multigenerational barrio tradition via a group known as the VCs.

20. E.g. El Circle, La Dot, Ghost Town, El Alto, La Tripa, Los Cassianos, La Blanca, Las Colonias, and others.

21. It is important to note that Montejano was not focused on barrio gang longevity, but rather on how former barrio gang members, and in some cases entire gangs, became politically radicalized in the Chicano movement and evolved into hardcore activist groups.

22. E.g., Barricas, El Detroit, El Hot Corner, Los Tigers, Los Osos, Vargas Cats, El Chicago.

23. A detailed section on the San Juan Homes and Varrio La Blanca appears in chapter 4.

24. Without estimates for various points in between the 1950s and 2007, one cannot be sure of the extent of fluctuations in the relative size of the gang population. Chapter 7 shows high gang prevalence rates for the late 1980s and early 1990s, for example.

25. Normally, an issue that complicates the counting of gang members is the fluidity of gang membership (Jacobs 2009). One's level of affiliation can range from wannabe to associate, to fringe, to core, which are all subject to change over time, based on one's age, experience, proven loyalties, etc. However, when the measurement is taken in retrospect, as in this study; i.e., when the population has aged and all has been "said and done," membership status becomes static and reliable. The methodology used to generate the 1950s lists of members, using saturation by multiple-subject confirmation of gang rosters in retrospect, also ensured the reliability of the estimate.

26. Clearly, not all of these are mutually exclusive categories, as some may occupy more than one of these statuses either simultaneously or at different stages in their lives.

27. In every study of this type, there is also a large proportion of offenders whose parents did not have criminal records.

28. Chapter 6 addresses the differences in values, organizational structure, and goals of modern Chicano gangs versus those of the 1940s and 1950s generations, and the resentment of those changes by elders.

29. An inmate-guard; a job typically offered to influential, respected inmates. While other inmates often resent these persons for their role, this particular subject "never had problems with that."

30. One notable exception in 1957 was the case of Fred Cruz, seventeen, who shot and killed Lupe Martinez, sixteen, in what appeared to be a disagreement over a girl who was present at the time of the shooting. The two boys had been incarcerated together at Gatesville (*San Antonio Light*, 1957(a)). To evidence the human capital potential of such an apparently violent barrio youth, Fred Cruz became a legally talented prison-rights activist as an inmate of the Texas prison system. His story and the prison reforms his efforts led to is told in an award-winning PBS documentary called "The Writ-Writer" (2007).

31. It is unknown what proportion of modern military enlistees are street gang members, but it is sure to be low, due to strict background checks barring felons from joining.

32. In the 1980s, the term "underclass" was coined to refer to the poorest of the poor in America who led a deviant, street-oriented lifestyle. It referred to a set of cultural and behavioral traits such as working age males not participating in the labor force, school dropout, and teen parenting, leading to households with many children headed by minority females on welfare. The underclass also experience multiple arrests for street-level criminality, problems with drug addiction, involvement with Child Protective Services, bearing children from multiple fathers, and men fathering children with multiple women.

33. In 2001, a four-year FBI probe of the San Antonio Police Department resulted in the arrest of eight officers who took part in both real and undercover (staged) drug trafficking operations. A similar case played out in San Antonio in 1980. The latest similar case involved a San Antonio area police officer (with the Balcones Heights Police Department) who was a confirmed member of the Texas Mexican Mafia (Contreras 2014).

34. In the academic literature on social stratification (social class), for adult subjects, human capital is measured mainly by education level, income, and occupational prestige, which is a slightly off point, but clearly related to the characterization offered here.

35. Chapter 6 offers more detailed information about the interplay of 1950s era gang members and their offspring who gravitated to prison gangs.

36. One exemplary casenote to demonstrate this is that of "Hippo," a former member of Taco Village who began injecting heroin at an early age and committing crimes to support this habit. At age nineteen, he enlisted in the army, only to return to street life after an honorable discharge, leading to a few terms in both state and federal prison. Several years later, he graduated with high honors (*Cum Laude*) in the social sciences from St. Edward's University in Austin, Texas. Hippo spent a lengthy career as a substance abuse professional and ultimately received gubernatorial and presidential pardons of his felonies, fully restoring his right to participate in all civic aspects of life.

37. *San Antonio Express-News,* "Oral History Project Collecting Stories about 1950s Gangs," by Karisa King. March 24, 2013. *The Texas Observer,* "Gangs of Old San Antonio," by Patrick Michels, August 8, 2013. Texas Public Radio's "The Source," with David Martin Davies, August 13, 2013.

38. A series of newspaper articles and expert panel discussions in 1940 and 1941 reflect long-held concerns with juvenile delinquency in San Antonio.

39. Like the Moonglow, the Butterfly was a bar in the Bounds with which there was an associated group of street boys in the 1940s and '50s. When the bar moved to the far West Side near Las Colonias barrio, the gang reemerged in that area (Erasmo, Calle Guadalupe).

40. Demolition completed in 2015.

41. Although separated by a creek, the Alazan and Apache housing projects have always been considered a single, sprawling tenement.

42. Unlike many other cities, which refer to their public housing developments as "projects" or "tenements", the term that caught on in the 1950s to refer to these areas in San Antonio was "the Courts". Although this was true of all public housing projects in San Antonio, "Los Courts" always refers to Alazan-Apache, perhaps because it is the oldest of the Chicano populated projects. All others are commonly referenced by their specific name.

43. Lapses in upholding these expectations such as a guy "*que se hace patras en un gang fight*" (who wimps out or fails to backup his buddies), was given "courte," a roughing-up and chastisement by other members of the group that would have a lasting effect on his reputation and perhaps a disassociation from the gang.

44. Subject-collaborators also reviewed and approved the author's selections for inclusion.

45. A few of the reputable guys.

46. El Con was the slang term given to a *tiendita* (corner store) located at El Paso and Cibolo Streets in the West Side. The location and the name of the street gang associated with it were derived from a large storefront sign in the shape of a soft-serve ice-cream cone, hence El Cón. Chapter 7 describes this gang's role in 1980s prison gang formation.

47. One of at least six "Borrados" in San Antonio's 1950s Barrio Scene. Pete Sloss and Alberto Garza were two other Borrados from the Courts. Such duplications are in contrast to today's street subculture as it evolved from the 1980s. Today, when there are two or more known youth gang members with the same "tagname" (streetname), it is common under modern street code to engage in a fistfight to determine who deserves to keep the name.

48. *Stacy Adams* brand, fancy, shiny, pointed dress shoes with thin shoelaces, customary in traditional *pachuco* urban style.

49. A 1955 newspaper article was written about the possible spread of pachuco-style gangs from LA to San Antonio. In it, a juvenile bureau officer named Robert "Bob" Ramirez explained that local barrio gangs are simply imitators of the style of dress, speech, and delinquent attitude, but that he wished they were actually more organized, like LA based gangs. The loose structure of barrio gangs here, he stated, offered anonymity and lack of accountability to leadership within the gang, making violence and retaliation difficult to investigate (*San Antonio Light*, 1955).

50. One of at least three *Kilas* ("Killers") citywide. Gonzales's notoriety was based on his being the son of the infamous *Guero Polvos*, a 1930s-1940s barrio dweller whose status as a rueda or successful drug trafficker was legendary, due in part to a *corrido* written about him by Los Alegres de Teran. In this ballad, Guero Polvos (Rodolfo Gonzales, Sr.) was said to have been shot by police in a bar on Guadalupe Avenue in 1948 for refusing to give up his gun. Interestingly, no archival newspaper material was ever located to corroborate the corrido's tale.

51. One of four *Jokas* (Jokers) citywide. Others were Joe Robledo of Taco Village, Joe Lopez of El Con, and Chale Guzman of the Bounds' Red-Light Shoeshine Stand. As the oldest of the four, the latter was perhaps the barrio's original Joka.

52. A related example of the ubiquity of blade-carrying among barrio youth was when, in 1955, Sgt. Salas of the SAPD Juvenile Bureau conducted a surprise raid and frisk of the popular west downtown dancehall the *Radio Club*, confiscating some seventy-five knives and blades of all kinds (*San Antonio Light* 1955).

53. Varrio Kenwood was the only known 1950s barrio gang to be composed of blacks and Latinos (see chapter 2) until a mixed-race gang formed in the Lincoln Courts in the late 1980s.

54. One of numerous Chicano youth belonging to the barrio gang subculture who had an Anglo last name. Other well-known youth in this category were brothers Eduardo ("Walo") and Henry Porter, Chito and Joe Baker, Eddie Ferguson, Richard Harrison, Robert Freeman, Pete Sloss, Vicente Stewart, Jake Zimmerle, Willie Hall, Rufus Johnson, Jack Barber, and Billy McDonald.

55. Others close to Guerrero and who did time with him say he wasn't much of an agitator in prison, but was ostentatious on the outside.

56. For example, narcotics detective Manuel Ortiz, who had barrio roots, and Felony Squad detective Bill Weilbacher, who did not, had an unfriendly rivalry that was likely exacerbated by this dynamic (McKinney 1975).

57. Most bar operators did not own the building where they ran the bar. In times of economic restructuring in the neighborhood, and/or at the whim of the buildings' owners, the building could be repurposed and the bar operator forced to relocate, often at his/her own expense.

58. This bar was a particular favorite among barrio clientele because Chota was known to be a barrio historian and archivist. His bar was adorned with old photos of places and people in the Bounds and the West Side that dated back to the 1930s.

59. Extortion by prison gangs especially becomes a concern among barrio bar owners as of the mid-1980s.

60. In his study of Chicano homicide in San Antonio, Martinez (2014) identified Guadalupe Street as the most deadly corridor in the West Side for the high number of murders, going back to the 1950s, that occurred either on it or near it.

61. Interestingly, La Dot and El Circle were rival gangs throughout the 1960s, echoing the theme in chapter 3 that narcotics dynamics have a way of transcending barrio alliance.

62. As of this writing, I await return correspondence from Huerta on this matter and on the influence of the Fred Carrasco group on *Eme* formation.

63. For example, Martinez (2014) noted that in the 1950s and 1960s era in San Antonio, 100 percent of Latinos murdered in the sixteen to twenty-four age group were male. No young Latinas were murder victims in this era, and few Latino children or elderly were murder victims.

64. In the Texas prison system, San Antonio gangs are a reputable, respected entity throughout the state. El Paso inmates also carry a reputation for ferocity. As of the late 1980s, a number of inmates from San Antonio acquired the tattoo "Most Hated," which in Texas's prison subculture, is understood to be San Antonio. Even in the most recent of political gang posturing in Texas jails and prisons, San Antonio and El Paso stand alone, while much of the rest of the state are allied under regional factions called Tangos (Tapia 2013; Tapia et al. 2014).

65. Membership in most Latino prison gangs is widely considered to be a lifelong commitment and most operate via a "blood-in-blood-out" oath, where a member who wishes to separate from the group may be marked for death. Due to factional splintering and discontent with group politics over time, however, a specific class of absconders known as *equis* (exes) have accumulated. Under typical prison gang rules, persons so classified would normally be "green-lighted" for elimination; however, such a critical mass has accumulated over time that in most cases, it has become impractical to apply this doctrine.

66. However, the 2015 Texas Gang Threat Assessment (an annual Texas Department of Public Safety report), still lists the Texas Mexican Mafia (TMM) and other Latino prison gangs as among the highest priorities for law enforcement.

67. Drug suppliers cannot take their distributors to civil claims court or seek criminal prosecution for failing to turn in profits or absconding with merchandise, for example.

68. Some of the most valued *caméos* (jobs) consist of assaulting rival gang members or members of one's own organization as a disciplinary measure.

69. As evidenced in recent jail and prison gang documentaries and as informally expressed to the authors by police and gang member sources.

70. One example from San Antonio's Tango is a much-talked-about renegade group known as *Nuestro Tango Orejón* (NTO), who have widely claimed aspirations to organize like a "familia" (i.e. Mafia).

71. It is not clear to this author where or when this informal title originated, but it is the most common phrase uttered in popular or professional discussions of youth gang violence in San Antonio. Bolden (2014) also alludes to this reputation in a similar context. It has even been used to justify the need for federal funds for youth gang intervention granted to the city by the Office of Juvenile Justice and Delinquency Prevention (OJJDP) in 1996.

72. It is not known whether SAPD used motive-based or documented member-based criteria to generate these estimates.

73. Aside from the LA Boyz, some of the BTK's most formidable enemies were the Raiders, the Ambrose, Tepa-13, and Bad Company, all of whom adopted the structure of the Chicago-based Folk nation, the avowed enemies of the People nation.

74. There was a genuine Latin Kings gang in San Antonio. They were Puerto Ricans with direct ties to those in Chicago, but they were a small group, distinct from the approximately one thousand Kings members of various homegrown San Antonio sets.

75. A group of twenty core Ambrose members were said to have migrated to San Antonio and established the gang in the early 1990s, but thereafter, the group splintered into the following factions due to infighting: Bristol Street Boys, Chicano Boyz, Denver Street Gangsters, Hunter Street Boys, McKinley Street Thugs, and Northside Ambrose. The larger group eventually reunited and like the VLB, had violent conflicts with prison gangs over drug-tax street politics in the early 2000s.

76. SAPD's method of generating active gang lists is peculiar and error prone. It appears that the main criteria for placing an individual in the active gang database is that s/he has been charged with a crime within the last five years for adults, two years for juveniles, and has claimed a gang either at the time of

arrest or in the past. The gang to which the individual belongs or belonged is then entered into a list of active gangs, each of which is accompanied by the number of current members from that gang that are also in the database.

77. The latter method is not as reliable as it once was because of changes in subcultural norms and the role of technology in gang cohesiveness. Today, younger members rely more on cell phones and online social networking to communicate than on regular, neighborhood-based face-to-face interaction.

78. For example, for a short time, a prison gang forced VLB to dissipate or at least drop their name. The group then adopted "West Side Posse" (WSP), which stuck, because when VLB reclaimed their name during the war with the prison gang, WSP was retained by the younger cohort.

79. Of those not already named above.

80. This group was said to be a California transplant, started up in San Antonio by Gordo in the far West Side area known as Las Colonias.

81. A Mirasol Courts gang.

82. Kubrin (2005) also points out how "crazy," unpredictably violent behavior is also valued by the ghetto's gangsta subculture.

83. This is an ethnocentric, group-loyalty based set of values that, for the last three decades in Texas, relies on a paramilitary hierarchy for its group structure.

84. Blue cardstock was used to keep these one-page, 8" x 11" gang-member profiles, which were cabinet filed and entered into an electronic database.

85. This is a list of terms and sayings mainly specific to South Texas, for which San Antonio is the largest city and hence, the likely originator of the term. It is a subset of a much larger cadence that is used in the barrios of Texas and most other Southwestern cities.

References

Anderson, E. 1994. "The code of the streets." *Atlantic Monthly* 273(5): 80–94.

Allen, Paula. 2009. "Basement where narcotics king gunned down long gone." *San Antonio Express-News*. March 22, 4-G.

Arguello, Javier. San Antonio Police Department Recruiter, Personal Communication, October 15, 2013.

Armaline, William, Vera-Sanchez, Claudio, and Mark Correia. 2014. "The Biggest Gang in Oakland: Rethinking Police Legitimacy." *Contemporary Justice Review,* Taylor & Francis, Online First.

Ball, Richard A. and G. David Curry. 1995. "The Logic of Definition in Criminology: Purposes and Methods for Defining 'Gangs.'" *Criminology,* 33(2): 225-245.

Barrows, Julie and Ronald Huff. 2009. "Constructing and Deconstructing Gang Databases." *Criminology and Public Policy,* 8(4): 675-701.

Bartlett, James E., Kotrlik, Joe W., and Chadwick C. Higgins. (2001). "Determining Sample Size in Sample Size in Survey Research." *Information Technology, Learning, and Performance Journal,* 19 (1): 43 – 50.

Batty, Elaine. 2009. "Reflections on the use of oral history techniques in social research." *People, Place & Policy Online,* 3(2): 109-121.

Bernburg, J. G., Krohn, M.D., & Rivera, C.J. (2006). "Official Labeling, Criminal Embeddedness, and Subsequent Delinquency: A Longitudinal Test of Labeling Theory." *The Journal of Research in Crime and Delinquency,* 43, 67-90.

Besemer, Sytske. 2012. "The impact of timing and frequency of parental criminal behaviour and risk factors on offspring offending." *Psychology, Crime, and Law, 1-22.*

Bjerregaard, B., and Alan J. Lizotte. 1995. "Gun Ownership and Gang Membership." *The Journal of Criminal Law and Criminology,* (86): 37-58.

Bogardus, E. 1943. "Gangs of Mexican American Boys." *Sociology & Social Science Research,* 28: 55-66.

Bolden, Christian. 2014. "Friendly Foes: Hybrid Gangs or Social Networking." *Group Processes and Intergroup Relations.* 17(6), 730-749.

Borgotti, Stephen. 2006. "Identifying sets of key players in a social network." *Computer Math Organizational Theory,* 12: 21-34.

Bowser, David. 2003. *West of the Creek: Murder, Mayhem, and Vice in Old San Antonio.* San Antonio, Texas: Maverick Publishing.

Brickman, A. M. and Stern, Y. 2009. "Aging and Memory in Humans." *Sage Encyclopedia of Neuroscience,* 1: 175-180.

Brotherton, David and Luis Barrios. 2004. *The Almighty Latin King and Queen Nation.* New York: Columbia University Press.

Bursik, Robert J. Jr. and Harold G. Grasmick. 1993. *Neighborhoods and Crime: The Dimensions of Effective Community Control.* New York: Lexington Books.

Burt, Callie, Sweeten, Gary, and Ronald Simons. 2014. "Self Control Through Emerging Adulthood: Instability, Multidimensionality, and Criminological Significance." *Criminology,* 52(3): 450-487.

Campbell, H. 2009. *Drug War Zone: Frontline Dispatches from the Streets of El Paso & Juarez.* Austin: UT Press.

Cancino, Jeffrey, Martinez, Ramiro, and Jacob Stowell. 2009. "Intra and Inter-Group Robbery: the San Antonio Experience." *The ANNALS of the Academy of Political and Social Science,* 623: 12-24.

Casillas, Victor. 1994. "Identifying and Supervising Individuals Affiliated with Community Threat Groups." *Federal Probation,* 53 (2): 11-19.

Castañola, Albert. 2015. Bexar County Juvenile Gang Unit Officer. Personal Communication, March 18.

Chambers, William T. 1940. "San Antonio, Texas." Economic Geography, 16(3): 291-298. Chambliss, William. 1994. "Policing the Ghetto Underclass," Social Problems, 41 (2): 177-194.

City of San Antonio. Ordinance 1320, Feb 26, 1940, Amended, OJ-26, Jan. 24, 1950.

City of San Antonio. 2014. Office of Cultural Affairs. "Cassiano Homes Murals." http://www.saculturaltours.com/spot.php?t=1&s=124 [accessed Sept. 20].

Cloward, Richard A. and Lloyd E. Ohlin. 1960. *Delinquency and Opportunity: A Theory of Delinquent Gangs.* New York: The Free Press.

Cohen, Albert. 1955. *Delinquent Boys.* Glencoe, IL. The Free Press.

Cohn, D'Vera. 2010. "Census History: Counting Hispanics." Pew Research Center online report, http://www.pewsocialtrends.org/2010/03/03/census-history-counting-hispanics-2/ [retrieved March 6, 2014].

Contreras, Guillermo. 2014. "Source: Slain Cop Suspected of Mexican Mafia Affiliation." *San Antonio Express-News,* May 13, p. 1-A.

Crouse, Jacque and Thomas Edwards. 1990. "Cocaine charges send parolee, called 'flunky,' back to prison." *San Antonio Express-News,* June 26, F-5.

Curry, David G. 2000. "Self-reported gang involvement and officially recorded delinquency." *Criminology,* 38(4): 1253-1273.

Curry, David G. and Scott Decker. 1997. "What's in a name? A Gang by any other name isn't quite the same." *Valparaiso University Law Review,* 31: 501-514.

Davenport, Joe. 1965. "Finding of Cortinas' Body Told." *San Antonio Express-News,* May 30, 5- A.

Davidson, Theodore. 1974. *Chicano Prisoners: The Key to San Quentin.* New York: Holt, Rinehart and Wilson.

Decker, Scott, and Barrick Van Winkle. 1996. *Life in the Gang.* Cambridge University Press.

Duff, Audrey, 1994. "'We Get All Hyped Up. We Do a Drive-by.': A report from the front lines of the San Antonio gang wars." *Texas Monthly.* October 1.

Dunn, Patricia. 1997. "The Cementville School: a study of education, labor, and segregation in a company town." Master's Thesis, St. Mary's University, San Antonio, Texas, 1-77.

Durán, Robert. 2012. *Gang Life in Two Cities: An Insider's Journey*. Columbia University Press.

Durán, Robert J. 2009. "Legitimated Oppression: Inner-city Mexican American Experiences with Police Gang Enforcement." *Journal of Contemporary Ethnography*, 38(2): 143- 168.

Dyer, John "Rocky" Det. San Antonio Police Department. 2015. Personal Communication, May 12.

Eddy, J. Mark and John B. Reed. 2001. "The Antisocial Behavior of the Adolescent Children of Incarcerated Parents: A Developmental Perspective." The Urban Institute Report, Working Paper, "From Prison to Home" Conference, Jan. 2002. Washington DC 1-26.

Eiserer, Tanya. 2008. "Texas' Tango Blast gang draws kids with tattoos, loose affiliation rules." *The Dallas Morning News*, November 30.

Eitle, David. Grunkel, Steven, and Karen Van Gundy. 2004. "Cumulative Exposure to Stressful Life Events and Male Gang Membership." *Journal of Criminal Justice*, 32(2): 95-111.

Esbensen, Finn-Aage, Thomas Winfree Jr., Ni He, and Terrance Taylor. 2001. "Youth Gangs and Definitional Issues: When is a Gang a Gang and Why Does it Matter?" *Crime and Delinquency*, 47: 105-130.

Fabelo, Tony, Michael D. Thomson, Martha Plotkin, Dottie Charmichael, Miner Marchbanks, and Eric Booth. 2011. "Breaking School's Rules: A Statewide Study [TX] of How School Discipline Relates to Students' Success and Juvenile Justice Involvement." Council of State Governments and the Public Policy Research Institute. July: 1-124.

Faust, Katherine. 2006. "Comparing Social Networks: Size, Density, and Local Structure." *Metodološki zvezki*, 3 (2), 2006: 185-216.

Farrington, David. 2011. "Families and Crime" in *Crime and Public Policy*. Wilson, J.Q. and J. Petersilia (Eds). Pp. 130-157. New York, Oxford University Press.

Federal Bureau of Investigation. 2002. *Supplemental Homicide Reports*. Washington DC: US Department of Justice.

Federal Bureau of Investigation. 2015. "Percent of Offenses Cleared by Arrest or Exceptional Means, 2012," http://www.fbi.gov/about-us/cjis/ucr/crime-in-the-u.s/2012/crime-in-the-u.s.-2012/offenses-known-to-law-enforcement/clearances [accessed April 3].

Fleisher, Mark. 1995. *Beggars & Thieves: Lives of Urban Street Criminals*. Madison: University of Wisconsin Press.

Flippen, Chenoa and Emilio A. Parrado. 2012. "Forging Hispanic Communities in New Destinations: A Case Study of Durham, NC." *City & Community*, 1:1-30.

Fong, Robert 1990. "The organizational structure of prison gangs: a Texas Case Study". *Federal Probation*, 54(1): 36-44.

Fong, Robert, Vogel, Ronald, and Salvador Buentello. 1992. "Prison Gang Dynamics: A Look Inside the Texas Department of Corrections." 57-77. In Benekos, P. and A. Merlo. (Eds). *Corrections: Dilemmas and Directions*. Cincinnati: ACJS Anderson.

Freedman, David A. 2002. *The Ecological Fallacy*. Berkeley: University of California.

Glass, James. 2014. Data Analyst, San Antonio Police Department, Personal Communication, May 8.

Gonzales-Baker, Susan. 1996. "Demographic Trends in the Chicana/o Population." *Chicanas/Chicanos at the Crossroads: Social, Economic, and Political Change*. Maciel, David, and Isidro Ortiz (ed.). University of Arizona Press, pp. 5-24.

Gottfredson, Michael and Travis Hirschi 1990. *A General Theory of Crime*. Palo Alto, CA: Stanford University Press.

Greene, J. and K. Pranis. 2007. "Gang Wars: The Failure of Enforcement Tactics and the Need for Effective Public Safety Strategies." Justice Policy Institute Report, 1-104.

Grogger, Jeffrey and Stephen J, Trevino. 2002. "Falling Behind or Moving Up?: The Intergenerational Progress of Mexican Americans." Research Brief, Public Policy Institute of California.

Hagedorn, John. 1988. *People and Folks: Gangs, Crime, and the Underclass in a Rustbelt City*. Chicago: Lakeview Press.

Holloway, Stephen R., Deborah Bryan, Robert Chabot, Donna M. Rogers, and James Rulli. 1998. "Exploring the Effect of Public Housing on the Concentration of Poverty in Columbus, Ohio." *Urban Affairs Review,* 33: 767-789.

Horowitz, Ruth. 1983. *Honor and the American Dream: Culture and Identity in a Chicano Community*. New Brunswick: Rutgers University Press.

Howell, James. 1999. "Youth Gang Homicide." *Crime and Delinquency* 45(2): 208-241.

Howell, James. 2001. "Youth Gang Programs & Strategies." Washington, DC, National Youth Gang Center.

Huff, C. Ronald. 1989. "Youth Gangs and Public Policy." *Crime and Delinquency,* 35: 524-37.

Hughes, Lorine. (2005). "Studying Youth Gangs: Alternative Methods & Conclusions." *Journal of Contemporary Criminal Justice,* 21(2): 98-119.

Hughes, Lorine. 2013. "Group Cohesiveness, Gang Member Prestige, and Delinquency and Violence in Chicago, 1959-1962." *Criminology, 51(2): 795-832.*

Isen, Joshua. 2010. "A meta-analytic assessment of Wechsler's P > V sign in antisocial Populations." *Clinical Psychology Review, 30 (4): 423-435.*

Jacobs, Bruce A. 2004. "A typology of street criminal retaliation." *Journal of Research in Crime and Delinquency,* 41:295-323.

Jacobs, James. 1974. Street Gangs behind Bars. *Social Problems,* 21: 395-409.

Jacobs, James. 2009. "Gang Databases: Context and Questions." *Criminology and Public Policy, 8(4): 705-709.*

Kennedy, David. 2009. "Constructing and Deconstructing Gang Databases." *Criminology and Public Policy,* 8(4): 710-716.

Klein, Malcolm. 1995. *The American Street Gang*. New York: Oxford University Press.

Knox, George, Houston, James, Tromanhauser, Ed, McCurrie, Tom, and John Laskey. 1996. "Addressing and Testing the Migration Issue: A Summary of Recent Findings," in *Gangs: A Criminal Justice Approach* (Miller, Mitch and Jeff Rush eds.) Cincinnati: ACJS/Anderson Monograph Series.

Kornhauser, Ruth. 1978. *Social Sources of Delinquency: Underlying Assumptions of Basic Models of Delinquency Theories*. Chicago: University of Chicago Press.

Kubrin, Charis. 2005. "Gangstas, Thugs, and Hustlas: Identity and the Code of the Street in Rap Music." *Social Problems,* 52(3): 360-378.

Laub, John, and Robert Sampson. 2003. *Shared Beginnings, Divergent Lives.* Cambridge, MA: Harvard University Press.

Lauritson, J. 1993. "Sibling resemblance in delinquency." *Criminology,* 31, 387-409.

Marquez, Raquel, Mendoza, Louis, and Steve Blanchard. 2007. "Neighborhood Formation on the West Side of San Antonio, Texas." *Latino Studies,* 5: 288-316.

Martinez, Ramiro. 2014. *Latino Homicide.* 2nd Edition. New York, Routledge.

Maxson, Cheryl L. 1993. "Investigating gang migration: contextual issues for intervention." *Gang Journal,* 1: 1-8.

Maxson, Cheryl L., Kristi J. Woods, and Malcolm W. Klein. 1996. "Street Gang Migration: How Big a Threat?" *National Institute of Justice Journal,* 230: 26-31.

Maxson, Cheryl, and Malcolm Klein. 2001. "Defining gang homicide: An updated look at member and motive approaches." In *The modern gang reader* (2nd ed.), ed. Jody Miller, Cheryl L. Maxson, and Malcolm W. Klein. Los Angeles: Roxbury.

McCord, Joan. 1991. "The Cycle of Crime and Socialization Practices." *Journal of Criminal Law & Criminology,* 82(1): 211-228.

McKinney, Wilson. 1975. *Fred Carrasco: The Heroin Merchant.* Austin, Texas: Heildelberg Publishing.

McNulty, Thomas L. and Stephen Holloway 2000. "Race, Crime, and Public Housing in Atlanta: Testing a Conditional Effect Hypothesis." *Social Forces, 79(2): 707-729.*

Mirandé, Alfredo. 1987. *Gringo Justice.* South Bend, Indiana, University of Notre Dame Press.

Moffitt, T. E. (2006). "Life-course persistent versus adolescence-limited antisocial behavior." In D. Cicchetti & D. Cohen (Eds.), *Developmental psychopathology,* (2nd ed., pp. 570- 598). New York, NY: Wiley.

Montejano, David 2010. *Quixote's Soldiers: A Local History of the Chicano Movement, 1966- 1981.* Austin, UT Press.

Moore, Joan. 1978. *Homeboys.* Philadelphia: Temple University Press.

Moore, Joan and Raquel Pinderhughes (eds.) 1993. *In the Barrios: Latinos and the Underclass Debate.* New York: Russell Sage Foundation.

Moore, J. Vigil, D. and A. Garcia. 1983. "Residence and Territoriality in Chicano Gangs." *Social Problems,* 31(2):182-94.

Moore, John and Reed Holland. 1973. "The Laredo-San Antonio Heroin Wars." *Texas Monthly,* August, 1 – 14.

Moreno, Mark E. 2006. "Mexican American Street Gangs, Migration, and Violence in the Yakima Valley" *Pacific Northwest Quarterly,* 97 (3): 131-138.

Morrill, Robert. 2007. *The Mexican Mafia, La Eme: The Story.* San Antonio, Texas: Mungia Printers.

Murdock, Steve, Michael E. Cline, Mary P. Zey, Wilner Jeanty, and Deborah Perez. 2013. *Changing Texas: The Implications of Addressing or Ignoring the Texas Challenge.* College Station, Texas: A&M University Press.

National Gang Intelligence Center. 2011. "National Gang Threat Assessment: Emerging Trends." Washington, DC, 1-100.

National Gang Intelligence Center. 2016. "National Gang Report 2015." Washington, DC, 1- 64.

Oelofse, Marietjie. 2011. "Applying Principles of Historical Critique: Authentic Oral History?" *International Conference on Social Science and Humanity*, IPEDR 5(2): 41-44.

Olguin, Ben. 2010. *La Pinta: Chicano Prisoners, Culture, and Politics*. Austin: University of Texas Press.

Osborn, S. G. and D. J. West (1979). "Conviction Records of Fathers and Sons Compared." *British Journal of Criminology*, 19(4): 120 – 133.

Papachristos, Andrew. 2013 "The importance of cohesion for gang research, policy, and practice." *Criminology & Public Policy, 12, 1: 51-61.*

Piquero, Alex and Timothy Brezina. 2001. "Testing Moffitt's Account of Adolescence-Limited Delinquency." *Criminology*, 39: 353-370.

Putnam, Robert. 2000. *Bowling Alone: The Collapse and Revival of American Community*. New York, Simon and Schuster.

Pyrooz David & Gary Sweeten. 2015. "Gang Membership Between Ages 5 and 17 Years in the United States." *Journal of Adolescent Health*, 56 (4): 414–419.

Pyrooz, David, Gary Sweeten, & Alex Piquero. 2013. "Continuity and Change in Gang Membership and Gang Embeddedness." *Journal of Research in Crime and Delinquency*, 50(2): 239-271.

Quinones, Sam. 2014. "The End of Gangs." *Pacific Standard*. Dec. 29, http://www.psmag.com/politics-and-law/the-end-of-gangs-los-angeles-southern-california-epidemic-crime-95498 [retrieved May 26, 2015].

Ricketts, Erol and Isabel V. Sawhill. 1988. "Defining and Measuring the Underclass." *Journal of Policy Analysis and Management*, 7(2): 316-325.

Roberts, David. 1960. "Teen Killing Leaves S.A. Families in Fear." *San Antonio Light*, June 25, 2-e.

Rodriguez, Nestor. 1993. "Economic Restructuring and Latino Growth in Houston," pp. 101- 127 in Moore, and Pinderhughes (eds.) *In the Barrios: Latinos and the Underclass Debate*. New York: Russell Sage Foundation.

Rosenthal, Lawrence. 2000. "Gang Loitering and Race." *Journal of Criminal Law and Criminology,* 91:99-160.

Ryan, Carol. San Antonio Police Department Recruiter, personal communication, Oct. 4, 2012. Sampson, R., Morenoff, J. and E. Raudenbush. 2005. "Social anatomy of racial and ethnic disparities in violence." *American Journal of Public Health*, 95(2): 225-32.

Sanders, Heywood. 2014. "San Antonio's Checkered Past: Where's the red-light district's historical marker?" *San Antonio Current,* January 22-28: 12.

San Antonio Evening News. 1920. "Guns, Boys, and Loot Taken in Raid by Police: Goods Concealed in Shack When Member of Gang Squeals." Jan. 19, p. 2.

San Antonio Express-News. 1939. "Judge Planning to Create Bexar County 'Boys Town.'" Jan. 15., p. A-4

San Antonio Express-News. 1940. "Less Juvenile Delinquency in Bexar County." July 16, p. 6

San Antonio Express-News. 1951(a). "Youth Admits Perjury, Fears Attacks in Jail." Aug. 1, p. 2

San Antonio Express-News. 1951(b). "Judge Gives DA Credit for Youth 'Gang' Inquiry". Aug. 5, p. 1.

San Antonio Express-News. 1952 (a). "Juvenile's Tattoo mark is mystery to court." January 28, p. 12.

San Antonio Express-News. 1952 (b). "Four Charged in Dope Raids." July 29, p. 1-B.

San Antonio Express-News. 1953. "Days of Gangs Believed Over in San Antonio," January 26, p. 1.

San Antonio Express-News. 1954. "Court Hangs Up Conviction Mark." May 29, p. 12-A.

San Antonio Express-News. 1955. "Youth Beaten by Youth Gang," p. 2-A.

San Antonio Express-News 1956 a. "Boy 16 Shot on Left Leg," Oct. 28, p. 14-A.

San Antonio Express-News 1956 b. "Youth Admits Post Office Knifing, Two Other Cuttings," June 15, p. 14-C.

San Antonio Express-News 1957. "Five Indicted in Shootings," April 24. p. 1

San Antonio Express-News 1958. "Grand Jury Indicts Four For Murder," Dec. 18, p. 8-C.

San Antonio Express-News 1959. "3 Indicted on Assault on Narcotics Agent." June 11, p. 8-C.

San Antonio Express-News 1963. "Man in Shooting Faces 3 Charges." July 27, p. 10-D.

San Antonio Express-News 1970. "Three Dead, Three Hurt: No Leads in Tavern Shootout." July 7, p. 8-D.

San Antonio Express-News 1973. "Indictments Name Two." June 23, p.1-C

San Antonio Express-News. 1989. "Police Say Deaths of 6 Not Connected." Oct. 8, p. E-1.

San Antonio Express-News 2009. "Injunctions Work Disbanding Gangs: Editorial." Sept. 1.

San Antonio Housing Authority. 2014. http://www.saha.org/ [accessed Sept. 20, 2014]

San Antonio Light. 1910. "Suspect Mexican Boys of Kellam Robbery," July 12, p. 3.

San Antonio Light. 1914. "Young Thieves Arrested: Seven Mexican Boys Charged with Stealing Furniture and Clothes," January 19, p.5.

San Antonio Light. 1940. "Woman Slashed in Affray at Bar." Nov. 14, p. 8-A.

San Antonio Light. 1942. "Suspect in S.A. Slaying Arrested." Aug. 17, p. 1 / 4.

San Antonio Light. 1949. "Early S.A. Alleys Still Functioning." May 22. p.1.

San Antonio Light. 1950. "West Side Gangs Scored." April 30, p. 27.

San Antonio Light. 1951. "TV in Bars Pitfall to Youth." March 30, p. 8-A.

San Antonio Light. 1955. "Cop Spikes Rugcutters." Jan. 13, p. 23.

San Antonio Light 1956 (a). "Gang War End Sought." July 16, p. 1.

San Antonio Light 1956 (b). "2 S.A. Youth Held in Teenager Stab Death." July 16, p. 7.

San Antonio Light. 1957 (a). "Teenager Slain, Youth Held." May 5, p. 1.

San Antonio Light. 1957 (b). "Boy Says Killing 'Nothing Personal.'" Dec. 24, p. 1

San Antonio Light. 1957 (c). "Youth Gets Life in Fatal Beating." Nov. 2, p. 3.

San Antonio Light. 1957 (d). "Boy Assessed Ten Year Term." June 11, p. 37

San Antonio Light. 1957 (e). "S.A. Pair Charged As Dope Peddlers." April 5, p. 18

San Antonio Light. 1957 (f) "Bexar Con Killed by Guard's Gun." Sept. 19, p. 38.

San Antonio Light. 1958. "12 Nabbed in Dope Roundup." Oct. 3, p. 1.

San Antonio Light. 1959 (a). "Boy Gives Up Gun." April 6, p. 13.

San Antonio Light. 1959 (b). "S.A. Dope Raids Snare 20." March 25, p. 1.

San Antonio Light. 1960. "No. 5 Booked in Gang Killing." May 30, p. 4.

San Antonio Light. 1961. "20 Year Sentence for Dope Possession." April 27.

San Antonio Light. 1961 (a). "Federal Jury Indicts 14 from SA." Sept. 7, p. 17.

San Antonio Light. 1962. "Ice House Fracas: 8 Jailed After Fight." March 30, p. 13.

San Antonio Light. 1964. "Testimony in Trial Ends." Nov. 17, p 4.

San Antonio Light. 1970. "20 Years for Robbery." March 10, p 8.

San Antonio Light. 1974. "Two Enter Guilty Pleas." March 1, p.8-A.

San Antonio Police Department. 2004. "The Status of Gangs in Our Community." City Manager's Report to Council, April 15.

San Antonio Police Department. 2007. Gang Unit Presentation Slides. September 1.

Sanchez-Jankowski, Martin. 1991. *Islands in the Street: Gangs and American Urban Society.* Berkeley: University of California Press.

Schott, Joe. 1958. "Circle Gang Terrorizes S.A. Southwest Side." *San Antonio Light.* April 9.

Short, James, and Fred Strodtbeck. 1965. *Group Process and Gang Delinquency.* Chicago: University of Chicago Press.

Sikes, Gini. 1997. *8-Ball Chicks.* New York: Doubleday.

Snyder, Howard. 2006. "Juvenile Arrests 2004." Washington, DC: US Department of Justice, Office of Juvenile Justice and Delinquency Prevention.

Spergel, Irving. 1990. "Youth Gangs, Continuity and Change." *Crime and Justice* 12: 171-275.

Spergel, Irving, Wa, Ming, and Rolando Sosa. 2005. "Evaluation of the San Antonio-Comprehensive Community-Wide Approach to Gang Prevention, Intervention and Suppression Program." Unpublished Report, US Department of Justice, Document#209189: 1-231.

Tapia, Mike. 2011. "U.S. Juvenile Arrests: Gang Membership, Social Class, and Labeling Effects." *Youth and Society,* 43(4):1407-1432.

Tapia, Mike. 2013. "Texas Latino Gangs and Large Urban Jails: Intergenerational Conflict and Issues in Management." *Journal of Crime and Justice,* Routledge Online.

Tapia, Mike. 2014. "Latino Street Gang Emergence in The Midwest: Strategic Franchising or Natural Migration?" *Crime and Delinquency, 60(4): 592-618.*

Tapia, Mike, Corey Sparks, and J. Mitchell Miller. 2014. "Texas Latino Prison Gangs: An Exploration of Generational Shift and Rebellion." *The Prison Journal,* 94(2): 159 - 179.

Texas Department of Health, Bureau of Vital Statistics. 1979. Certificate of Death, State File #91073.

Texas Department of Health, Bureau of Vital Statistics. 1980. Certificate of Death, State File #32139.

Texas Department of Health, Bureau of Vital Statistics. 1981. Certificate of Death, State File #87661.

Texas Department of Public Safety 2011. "Texas Gang Threat Assessment 2011." Texas Fusion Center, Intelligence and Counter Terrorism Division: 1 – 60.

Texas Department of Public Safety 2015. "Texas Gang Threat Assessment 2015." Joint Crime Information Center, Intelligence and Counter Terrorism Division: 1 – 57.

Texas State Historical Association. 2014. "Alazan-Apache Courts." http://www.tshaonline.org/handbook/online/articles/mpa01 [retrieved on Sept. 19, 2014].

Thrasher, Frederic M. 1936. *The Gang,* 2d ed. Chicago: University of Chicago Press.

Tienda, Martha and Faith Mitchell. (eds.) 2006. *Hispanics and the Future of America.* National Research Council, Panel on Hispanics in the US National Academies Press: Washington, DC.

Tripplett, Ruth, 1997. "Youth Gangs in Texas, Part II." Texas Law Enforcement Management and Administrative Statistics Program. 4 (4): 1-11.

University of Texas at San Antonio Libraries Special Collections. 1996. Albert A. Peña, Jr. Papers, MS 37, Early Life Interview, http://digital.utsa.edu/cdm/singleitem/collection/p15125coll9/id/8083

US Census. 2014. Population Division, County Characteristics Resident Population Estimates, http://www.census.gov/cps/data/cpstablecreator.html [retrieved Jan 5, 2014].

US Census. 2015(a). Tiger Line with Selected Demographic and Economic Data. http://www.census.gov/geo/maps-data/data/tiger-data.html [retrieved Feb. 10].

US Census. 2015(b). Population of Counties by Decennial Census: 1900 to 1990. http://www.census.gov/population/cencounts/tx190090.txt [retrieved March 2]

US Department of Housing and Urban Development. 1984. "Evaluation of the Urban Initiatives Anti-Crime Program: San Antonio, Texas Case Study." Police Foundation Report, JFK School of Government, 1-30.

Valdez, Al and Rene Enriquez. (2011). *Urban Street Terrorism: The Mexican Mafia and the Sureño Trece.* Santa Ana, CA: Police and Fire Publishing.

Valdez, Avelardo. 1993. "Persistent Poverty, Crime, and Drugs: U.S. Mexican Border Region." Pp. 173-194 in Moore and Pinderhughes (eds.) *In the Barrios: Latinos and the Underclass Debate.* New York: Russell Sage Foundation.

Valdez, Avelardo. 2005. "Mexican American Youth and Adult Prison Gangs in a Changing Heroin Market." *Journal of Drug Issues,* 35 (4): 843 – 868.

Valdez, Avelardo. 2007. *Mexican American Girls and Gang Violence: Beyond Risk.* New York: Palgrave Macmillan.

Valdez, Avelardo, C. D. Kaplan, and E. Codina. 2000. "Psychopathy among Mexican American gang members: A comparative study." *International Journal of Offender Therapy and Comparative Criminology,* 44(1), 46-58.

Valdez, Avelardo and Steven J. Sifaneck. (2004). "Getting High and Getting by: Dimensions of Drug Selling Behaviors among American Mexican Gang Members in South Texas." *Journal of Research in Crime and Delinquency,* 41(1), 82-105.

Valdez, Avelardo, Alice Cepeda and Charles Kaplan. (2009). "Homicidal Events Among Mexican American Street Gangs: A Situational Analysis." *Homicide Studies,* 13: 288- 306.

Valdez, Raul Roy. n.d. "Chicano Gangs from 1950 to 1960." Unpublished paper, 1-12.

Vargas, Robert. 2014. "Criminal Group Embeddedness And The Adverse Effects Of Arresting A Gang's Leader: A Comparative Case Study." *Criminology,* 52(2): 143-168.

Vigil, James Diego. 1988. *Barrio Gangs: Street Life and Identity in Southern California.* Austin: Texas University Press.

Vigil, James Diego. 1990. "Cholos & Gangs: Culture Change and Street Youth in L.A." pp. 116- 128 in Huff (ed.) *Gangs in America.* New York: Sage.

Waldorf, Dan. 1993. "When the Crips Invaded San Francisco: Gang Migration." *The Gang Journal* 1: 11-16.

Western, Bruce. 2006. *Punishment and Inequality in America.* New York: Russell Sage Foundation.

Whyte, William Foote. 1943. *Street Corner Society: The Social Structure of an Italian Slum.* Chicago: University of Chicago Press.

Wilson, William J. 1996. *When Work Disappears: The World of the New Urban Poor.* New York, NY: Alfred A. Knopf.

Wolfgang, Marvin, Terrence Thornberry, and Robert Figlio. 1987. *From Boy to Man: From Delinquency to Crime.* Chicago: University of Chicago Press.

Womer, Sarah, and Robert Bunker. 2010. "Sureños Gangs and Mexican Cartel Use of Social Networking Sites." *Small Wars and Insurgencies,* 21(1): 81-94.

Yablonski, Lewis. 1959. "The Delinquent Gang as a Near-Group." *Social Problems,* 7, 108-117.

Yearwood, Douglass, and Alison Rhyne. 2007. "Hispanic/Latino Gangs: A Comparative Analysis of Nationally Affiliated and Local Gangs." *Journal of Gang Research* 14: 1-18.

Young, Renita. 2012. "In Chicago, Summer is Murder Season." *The Grio,* http:// thegrio.com/2012/06/01/in-chicago-summer-is-murder-season/ #s:chicago-murders-2 [Accessed on September 1, 2014].

Zats, Marjorie. 1987. "Chicano youth gangs and crime: the creation of a moral panic." *Contemporary Crisis,* 11(2): 129-158.

Zelman, Donald L. 1983. "Alazan-Apache Courts," *Southwestern Historical Quarterly,* 87(2): 123 –150.

Index

About the Author

Mike Tapia is an assistant professor of criminal justice at New Mexico State University. His teaching and research interests include crime theory, race, and street crimes. He has published work on Latino gang migration and on risk factors in juvenile and Latino arrest. Mike was born in El Paso, Texas, and received a PhD in Sociology from Ohio State University.

www.ingramcontent.com/pod-product-compliance
Lightning Source LLC
Chambersburg PA
CBHW020533270326
41927CB00006B/550